Lynching in the American Press

The 1900s

By
Joe Mitchell

The reader will find newspaper accounts published from Northern, Southern, African American, White, Democratic, and Republican newspapers within this volume. Many articles found in this book are presented verbatim, as they appeared in the original press reports, while some of the reports have been drastically revised or corrected for the sake of clarity and readability. However, in no case have any details or facts been altered as reported by the press. In cases where several articles contained different of conflicting information, each article has been published. With the exception of a few excerpt passages from several books, personal letters, and magazines, most of the reports are printed in their entirety.

J. H. Mitchell

MARIETTA DAILY LEADER
March 25, 1900

A DOUBLE LYNCHING. O'GRADY, A WHITE MAN, AND COTTON, COLORED, MURDERERS, PUT TO DEATH BY MOBS.

RICHMOND, Va., March 25.—The negro who, with a white man, killed Justice of the Peace Saunders and Mr. Welton, at Skippers, Thursday, was, after an all-night chase, captured at Stoney Creek, Sussex County. He confessed to the shooting of Saunders and Welton and to several robberies. He is the notorious negro, Cotton.

The negroes of Greensville Saturday lynched O'Grady, the white man who was with Cotton, the negro, when he killed Saunders and Welton. Cotton was lynched earlier in the day by a mob of white men.

THE (BOSTON) INDEPENDENT
May 31, 1900

TWO LYNCHINGS.

OF all crimes the most criminal are those that attack law in the execution of its duties. Such a crime was one which last week brought dishonor to the State of Colorado, and another which occurred the week before in Georgia.

A negro had murdered two girls in Pueblo, Col. He escaped to Denver, but was there arrested and taken back to Pueblo. We will allow that he was guilty, although there is no legal evidence of it. On the arrival of the train in Pueblo a mob was waiting with ropes to hang him. His captors, so the dispatch says, instead of protecting him, pushed him out of the car door into the hands of the mob, who instantly put a noose about his neck and dragged him to a telegraph pole, where he was hanged. The Mayor, we are glad to say, called for order, but in vain. The accused would have had justice, if he had been tried; but a mob cares nothing for law, only for vengeance. Murder is barbarism, whether it be murder by an individual or murder by a mob. The former may indicate only a sporadic moral degeneracy; but the latter is the indictment of a whole community. We mention this case of lynching first, and with especial detestation, because it occurred in a Northern State.

The week before a case of lynching occurred in Augusta, Ga., where the relations between the two races had been rather pleasant. We tell a part of the story not from the papers, which gloss it all they can, but from private information. A young man, a student in a colored institution, dressed in the school uniform of an officer, accompanied by a colored lady teacher, entered a streetcar.

The pretension of a uniform is not liked by the whites, and when the two attempted to take a seat, a young white man, Whitney, and the lady with him spread themselves to shut them out. The woman crowded past them, and sat down in a colored woman's lap, when Whitney called out, "Don't let that wench sit on you." The colored man now sat down, crowding Whitney, who struck him, and tried to get him off the car. Here a colored man, Wilson, in the seat in front, said: "Don't go; stay on the car."

Then Whitney cursed Wilson and struck him with his fist, when Wilson rose as if to strike back. Whitney made a movement as if to draw a pistol, but Wilson drew first and shot Whitney through the head. Wilson was immediately seized, disarmed, beaten and turned over to the police, who locked him in jail, the Presbyterian minister appearing on the scene to prevent his being lynched. The white Democratic Primary was to be held in three days, and threats were made that if the sheriff would not let the crowd lynch Wilson he would not be re-nominated.

The papers say the negro was put on the cars, to be taken to Atlanta, and that a mob seized him from the train fifteen miles out. We are informed that he was not put on the train, but was taken out where the mob wanted him, and was killed, having first been tortured and mutilated beyond recognition. Portions of his body were carried off as souvenirs, and the rope was divided among the participators, many of whom are well enough known, and, like Whitney, are members of Christian churches.

A negro organization recovered Wilson's body, and an immense crowd attended the funeral, where all the colored pastors took part, counseling forbearance. They would not allow the coffin to be opened. The City Council immediately passed an ordinance confining negroes to the rear seats in cars. The sheriff was re-nominated the day after the lynching by a good majority. Such is the dispassionate story. This was no case of the "usual crime," but what would have been a "fracas between gentlemen," but for the fact that one was colored.

Why should those men have carried firearms? Why should not the ordinary processes of law have been observed? Is civilization, is education, is Christianity a failure? Certainly not. We do not at all despair, for the right must conquer in the end; but it will conquer only by the process, which holds law sacred and honors equally the rights of all men.

NEW YORK TIMES
July 23, 1900

THE GRAND JURY'S VERDICT. IT DECLARED THE ITALIANS LYNCHED HAD FORMED A CONSPIRACY.

TALLULAH, La., July 22.—The Grand Jury, which investigated the lynching of five Italians here yesterday, reported last night as follows: "It is evident from the facts brought to our knowledge that the men who were lynched had formed a conspiracy to assassinate Dr. Hodges, and the mob, learning of the facts, took the law into their own hands. After diligent inquiry, we have not been able to learn the names or identity of any of the men composing the mob."

The five Italians who were lynched had been living in Madison Parish for some years, and had filed their declarations to become citizens. Some had applied for naturalization papers.

COLORED AMERICAN (Washington, D.C.)
August 25, 1900

LYNCH LAW AND MISCEGENATION.

In view of the fact that there are so few charges of criminal assault against Negroes in the North where there are no miscegenation laws, and so very many in the South where such laws are the rule, a pertinent question, and one worth or serious consideration and discussion, is, what relation does lynch law bear to the law of miscegenation? It is an aspect of the question, which cannot be ignored by those who are seeking the truth. White men having license to do as the please with black women; while black men are lynched for looking at white women. There should be no miscegenation law in any state of the republic.—*New York Age.*

NEW YORK TIMES
August 30, 1900

HELPED TO LYNCH HIMSELF.

[Special to The New York Times]

NEW ORLEANS, Aug. 29.—A negro was lynched at Cheneyville, this State, this morning, the affair being attended by some original features. At 2 o'clock A.M. Alan Jackson, a popular young man of the neighborhood, was assassinated. Suspicion was directed to Tim Amos, a negro. A small party of white men found him at home in bed half an hour after the crime was committed. He was taken to the spot where Jackson fell, and there made a full confession, saying he had waited a long time for an opportunity to kill the young man.

The negro said he had anticipated being lynched for it, and offered to tie the rope around his own neck, climb a tree, tie the rope to a limb, and hang himself, thus sparing the lynchers the trouble. A vote on the proposition was taken, and the mob decided this would be an infringement on their rights and privileges. However, the negro was allowed to assist in the proceedings. The negro appeared to be in the best of spirits going up to the moment of death. After his death struggles had ceased the body was riddled with bullets.

NEW YORK TIMES
September 25, 1900

HATFIELD BURGLAR CAUGHT. FOUR MEN LYNCHED HAD NOTHING TO DO WITH CRIME.

NEW ORLEANS, Sept. 24.—The real Hatfelder burglar, the negro who caused the quadruple lynching at Ponchatoula, in "Bloody" Tangipahoa Parish, last Friday night, is in custody, and has been identified beyond question of doubt. To take no chances in the matter of identification, Sheriff Mix placed the negro, whose name is "Johnny" Lemon, in front of the little hotel. Without knowledge of the arrest, Mrs. Hatfield passed down the street with her husband. She saw the negro and screamed. "There he is, the negro who robbed us." The negro was moved under a strong guard to Amite City for safekeeping.

The officers announced that there will be no more lynchings at this time in the parish, provided no more outrages are committed. The four negroes lynched last Friday had no connection whatever with the Hatfelder robbery, but the argument is made in extenuation that the community is better off, and the negroes are where they can do no harm.

CARBONDALE (IL) FREE PRESS
October 5, 1900

NEGRO'S AWFUL PUNISHMENT. SOUTHERN MOB BY BALLOT BURN A BLACK RAVISHER AT THE STAKE.

Wetumpka, Ala., Oct. 3.—Winfield Townsend, alias Floyd, a negro, was burned at the stake in the little town of Eclectic, 15 miles from this place, yesterday. The negro's crime was an attempted assault on Mr. Lonnie Harrington, whose husband set fire to the fuel, which reduced Townsend's body to ashes.

SAN FRANCISCO (CA) CALL
November 17, 1900.

DEATH AT THE STAKE. THE AWFUL FATE OF A COLORADO GIRL-SLAYER.

LIMON, Colorado, Nov. 16.—Chained to a railroad rail set firmly in the ground, on the exact spot where his fiendish crime was committed, Preston Jr., or as he was familiarly known, John Porter, this evening paid a terrible penalty for his deed. It was 6:23 o'clock when the father of the murdered girl touched the match to the fuel, which had been piled around the negro, and twenty minutes later a last convulsive shudder told that life was extinct. What agony the doomed boy suffered while the flames shriveled up his flesh, could only be guessed from the terrible contortions of his face, and the cries he gave from time to time.

The executioners, who numbered about 300 citizens of Lincoln County, had not the least semblance of the ordinary mob. Their every act was deliberate and during all the preparations as well as throughout the sufferings of the negro hardly an unnecessary word was spoken. Grimly they stood in a circle about the fire until the body was entirely consumed, and then quietly they took their way back to Limon, whence they departed for their homes shortly afterward.

Preston Porter did not seem to realize the awful punishment that he was destined to undergo. As he had exhibited indifference to the enormity of his crime, so he seemed to lack all understanding of its terrible consequences. For more than an hour, while preparations for his execution were in progress, he stood mute and sullen among the avengers. When everything was ready he walked to the stake with a firm step, pausing as he reached the circle of broken boards to kneel and pray. He was allowed to take his time. He arose and placed his back to the iron stake and half a dozen men wound chains about his body and limbs. Kerosene oil was applied to the wood and after a brief pause Richard W. Frost, the father of little Louise Frost, whose cruelly mutilated body was found one week ago on that very spot, took his match safe out, extracted a match, lit it, and touched the flame to the oil.

For a moment only a little flickering flame arose, then the oil blazed up, sparks flew into the air and the wood began to crackle. Almost instantly the negro's trousers caught fire. Even though the flesh must have been scorched, he did not utter a sound. The flames crept upward on his clothing; the sparks flew up into a cloud of pale smoke. Porter turned his head and a frightful expression changed his face. With a sudden convulsive tugging he stretched his head as far from the rapidly increasing flames as possible, and uttered a cry of appeal. "Oh my God, let me go men. I've got something more to tell you. Please let me go; oh, my God, my God." In terrible screeches these words, the first he had uttered aloud, came from the negro.

A terrible tugging at the chains, a succession of awful moans and screams—the negro's awful agony was at last breaking down his sullen composure. Not an oath escaped him, but he begged and pleaded to be shot. Suddenly the rope holding his hands burned through. Then the arms, head, and shoulders slipped through the chain. For an instant the body stood erect, the arms were raised in supplication, while burning pieces of cloth dropped from them. The body then fell away from the fire, the head lower than the feet, which were still fastened to the rail. This was the end, and after a few moments the stolid men were disconcerted.

They feared that the only remaining chain would give way. If this had occurred the partly burned human being would have dashed among them with burning garments. Not many would have cared to capture him again. But the chain held fast. The body was then in such a position that only the legs were in the fire. The cries of the wretch were in redoubled, and he again begged to be shot. Some wanted to throw him over into the fire; other tried to throw oil upon him. Boards were carried and a large pile mad over the prostrate body. They were soon ignited, and the terrible heat and lack of air quickly rendered the victim unconscious, bring death a few moments later. The terrible ceremony out on the rolling prairie concluded the second tragedy upon that spot—the terrible vengeance of the first.

Through the entire affair little was said. As they had calmly prepared for the vengeance, so that people of the eastern part of the State carried out their plans, coolly and deliberately. There was not a hitch in the entire proceedings. Not a weapon was drawn. There was no angry discussion, and after the fire burned low they bade each other goodnight and went home. They did not stop to discuss the affair.

SAN FRANCISCO (CA) CALL
November 17, 1900.

LOUSE FROST'S FATHER DECIDES UPON BURNING. SUGGESTIONS OF MUTILATION ARE NOT HEEDED BY THE PARENT OF THE MURDERED CHILD.

The train bearing the Negro, in custody of Sheriff Freeman and his deputies, from Denver arrived in Limon at 3:45 p.m. It was at first announced that the Negro was to be executed by hanging. Many, including the father of the Negro's victim, protested that such a death would be too easy, and it was finally decided to leave the method of death to the outraged father. He decided upon burning at the stake. About three miles from Limon, and near the scene of the Negro's crime, the whole party left the train and began preparations for the deed of vengeance. Suggestions of mutilation before burning were made, but Mr. Frost declared against it.

Wagons were dispatched for wood, and upon their return, a score of men assisted in preparing it for the fire. When at last preparations were completed, a further delay was made, because it was known many were en-route from Hugo and other parts of the county to take part in the affair. It had been announced that 5:30 would be the hour for starting the fire, but it was nearly an hour later when the word was finally given.

A strange feature of the affair was that of souvenirs. The negro had since his confession been devoting every moment of daylight to the perusal of a Bible given to him by the Denver Jailer. Even while waiting for his execution he sat by a bonfire reading from the Gospel of St. Luke. Just before he was tied to the stake, upon requests for souvenirs, the boy tore the leaves from the Bible and distributed them among his executioners.

CAPITAL PUNISHMENT MAY AGAIN BE LEGALIZED IN COLORADO AS A RESULT OF PORTER'S CRIME

Meeting of Business Men and Clergy to Be Held at Denver and Colorado Springs to Protest Against the Burning of the Negro Criminal.

PRESTON (JOHN) PORTER JR., THE MURDERER OF LOUISE FROST, WHO WAS BURNED AT THE STAKE BY A MOB OF COLORADO CITIZENS AFTER HE HAD CONFESSED. REPRODUCED FROM A LIFE STUDY MADE BY A DENVER TIMES ARTIST.

[1]

---

[1]Picture of lynched African American named Preston Porter. Taken from *The San Francisco Call,* November 18, 1900.

LOUISE FROST, ALLEGED VICTIM OF JOHN PORTER,[2]

---

[2] *SAN FRANCISCO CALL*, November 17, 1900.

ROBERT W. FROST, LOUISE FROST'S FATHER.[3]

[3] *SAN FRANCISCO CALL*, November 17, 1900.

SAN FRANCISCO CALL, November 17, 1900.

BURNING AT THE STAKE OF PRESTON (JOHN) PORTER JR.

PRESTON (JOHN) PORTER JR., THE NEGRO BURNED AT THE STAKE AT LIMON, COLO. FROM A PHOTOGRAPH TAKEN IN DENVER ON THE DAY OF HIS ARREST.

***THE SAN FRANCISCO CALL.*, NOVEMBER 19, 1900, PG. 2 "PRESTON (JOHN) PORTER JR., THE NEGRO BURNED AT THE STAKE AT LIMON, COLO. FROM A PHOTOGRAPH TAKEN IN DENVER ON THE DAY OF HIS ARREST.**

SAN FRANCISCO CALL
November 17, 1900.

WOMEN VOTED FOR BURNING. WANTED NO MERCY SHOWN TO THE MURDERER OF LOUISE FROST.

LIMON, Colorado, Nov. 17.—The iron rail to which John Porter was bound will be left standing as a warning to all incline to deed similar to that for which young Porter was burned. A mound of earth has been piled up around the iron rail, covering the ashes, and it will remain as a monument in sight of all passing trains.

It is estimated that 700 persons witnessed the execution. No women remained during the cremation, but many of them went to the scene before the fire was lighted, and the negro was led from carriage to carriage for inspection. The women's vote was a unit for burning.

THE BEE (EARLINGTON, KY)
November 29, 1900

THE PORTER CREMATION. LEGAL PROCEEDING WOULD BE FUTILE.

DENVER, Colorado, Nov. 27.—The *Rocky Mountain News* prints the reply of Sheriff Freeman of Lincoln County, to the letter of District Attorney McAllister of Colorado Springs, Col., concerning the prosecution of the persons who burned the negro murderer, Preston Porter, at the stake at Limon, Col., recently.

After telling of how he was influenced into taking Porter from Denver to Limo upon the assurance of leading citizens of Lincoln County that he would be allowed to pass through Limo unmolested to Hugo, where he would be permitted to place Porter in the county jail. Sheriff Freeman declares that it would be impossible to get a jury in Lincoln or any adjoining county that would convict anyone charged with participation in the burning of Preston Porter. He concludes as follows:

"I do not justify the cremation, but I do object to having you and Governor Thomas saddle the blame of this burning on me, and I will not involve Lincoln County in a needless and fruitless litigation against its own citizens, or give additional advertisement to the state of Colorado for the sole purpose of making, as it seems to me, political capital for somebody"

"I want to add that politics cut no ice in this affair. While Lincoln County is a Republican county, the men who participated in his lynching were representatives of all political parties. When it comes to administering death to a brute who first assaults a child and then stabs and kicks her to death, I take it that true Americans lose sight of mere politics and remember only that they are fathers and brothers. It seems to me that we would be better off to let this episode rest where it now is."

BROWNSVILLE DAILY NEWS
December 11, 1900

RECOMMENDS INDEMNITY. A MEXICAN WAS LYNCHED IN LA SALLE COUNTY, TEXAS.

Washington, December 7.—In relation to the lynching in La Salle County, Texas, on October 5, 1895 of Florentino Suaste; a Mexican citizen, the president, in a special message to the senate today, recommended that the Mexican government be paid $2000 for the heirs of the victim. The recommendation made from motives of humanity and, "without reference to the question of liability of the government of the United States."

WATERLOO (IOWA) DAILY COURIER
December 21, 1900

LYNCHED THE WRONG NEGRO. INFURIATED MOB WREAKS VENGEANCE ON INNOCENT MAN.

[From The Associated Press.]

GULFPORT, Miss., Dec. 21.—Henry Lewis, the alleged negro murder of Marshall Richardson, has not yet been caught, although bloodhounds and a posse are still after him. The negro Lewis, who was lynched here yesterday by a mob, it now appears, was the cousin of the alleged murderer, and was wholly innocent of the crime.

ANACONDA (MONTANA) STANDARD
December 21, 1900

LYNCHED THE WRONG NEGRO.

MISTAKES will happen in the best-regulated families, likewise, in the most business-like mob of lynchers. What body of men is infallible? Even so wise an aggregation of individuals as the Massachusetts legislature passed a bill in which there was a misplaced semicolon, the misplacement resulting in the establishment of 11 p.m., instead of 1 a.m. as had been intended, as the hour for closing all the saloons in Massachusetts. With so conspicuous a precedent, he is a carping critic who would blame the Gulfport Mississippi assemblage of lynchers who yesterday, in their zeal and enthusiasm, lynched the wrong negro. Ignorance of the law does not exempt the mob from the law. Any man is liable to mistake one man for another, especially if he is not acquainted with either.

It was enough for the Gulfport mob to know that a white man had been murdered, and that a black man accordingly must be lynched. Business was business, and the mob had no time to spend on such trivial details as the murderer's identity. In baseball, the player who takes chances is a desired asset, even if he does make occasional errors. The same rule holds generally. To err is human; not inhuman; and more or fewer errors are expected all along the line. The blunder of the mob aroused the press to the acts of the lynchers. Blunders, therefore have a useful, and sometimes notable purpose in the world.

At most, the error of the Gulfport gentlemen was of a negative character, and in Mississippi, communities will redound to their credit.

WASHINGTON POST
January 11, 1901

WAITING FOR WHITES TO ATTACK. ARMED NEGROES GUARDING HOUSE OF MAN WHO WAS ORDERED TO LEAVE TOWN.

INDIANAPOLIS, Jan. 10.—The sequel to an attempt made by a mob of white men to drive from Newburg, Warrick County, a negro whose wife is alleged to be a white woman, may be an attempt to lynch the negro. The negro moved into the village a few days ago. The report that his wife was a white woman aroused indignation, and he was ordered to leave. He refused to obey the order, and a crowd of thirty or forty whites went to his house and commanded him out. The negro fired at the whites, and the shooting became general. Sixty shots were fired, but nobody was wounded. The mob finally retired.

The sheriff of Warrick County went to the scene of the trouble, and unsuccessfully urged the negro to leave, the latter declaring he would stay in his house. The negroes of Newburg have congregated at the cabin, heavily armed expecting an attack.

NORFOLK WEEKLY NEWS-JOURNAL
January 18, 1901

BURNED AT THE STAKE. FRED ALEXANDER LYNCHED BY MOB AT LEAVENWORTH.

LEAVENWORTH, Kansas, Jan 16.—Fred Alexander, the negro who Saturday evening attempted to assault Miss Eva Roth, and who was supposed to have assaulted and killed Pearl Forbes, in this city last November, was yesterday afternoon taken from jail and burned at the stake at the scene of his crime, six blocks from the center of the city. Probably 8,000 people witnessed the lynching. The wretch protested his innocence to the last.

Alexander was brought to the city from the penitentiary at Lansing at 4:30 p.m., and placed in the county jail. The citizens gathered in great numbers, and finding peaceable entrance to the jail impossible, armed themselves with railroad irons. The jail doors were battered down, and Alexander dragged to the scene of his crime, followed by hundreds of howling, frenzied men and boys. Once they arrived at the scene, a railroad rail was stuck into the ground, and the negro fastened to it with chains. Then coal oil was poured over his body.

Before the match was applied, John Forbes, the father of the murdered girl, stepped up to Alexander and said:

"Are you guilty of murdering my daughter?"

"I don't know what you have me here for," said the doomed man.

Forbes replied: "For killing my girl on this very spot."

"Mr. Forbes, if that's your name, you have the wrong man."

"Burn him, burn him," cried the crowd.

"Gentlemen, you have got lots of time," said Alexander.

"You're burning an innocent man. You took advantage of me. You gave me no show [trial]. Can I see my mother?"

A man in the crowd called for the mother, but she was not in the crowd. Alexander then said:

"Will you let me shake hands with all my friends?"

"You have no friends in the crowd, you damned beast," said one of the men in charge of the negro. "If you have anything to say, do so in a hurry."

Another man stepped up and said to Alexander: "Make your peace with your God, nigger, for you will surely die."

FORBES APPLIES THE MATCH.

Coal oil was then applied for the second time, and while it was being done, Alexander called to friends in the crowd, and told them good-bye. He did not seem to realize that he was to be burned at the stake, and talked rationally until John Forbes, the father of the murdered girl, lighted the match.

Again, Alexander was asked to make a confession, but he replied that he had nothing to say. As the flames leaped about him, Alexander turned ghastly pale, and for the first time realized that his death was near. He clasped his hands together, and began to swing to and fro while the crowd yelled. In less than five minutes he was hanging limp and lifeless by the chains that bound him.

As soon as the crowd saw that life was extinct, it began to slowly disperse. There were hundreds of the morbid, however, who stayed to the last. Men kept pilling on wood all the time, until about 7 o'clock, when the flames were allowed to die down. From 6 until 8 o'clock, there was a continuous stream of people going to the scene of the burning. These were persons who had been unable to get away from their work in the afternoon, but were determined not to miss seeing the awful spectacle.

When the fire had died down sufficiently to allow the crowd to approach what remained of Alexander, there was a wild scramble to obtain relics, bits of charred flesh, pieces of bone, scraps of wood, everything that could possible serve as a souvenir was seized on with morbid eagerness. The remains were viewed by thousands, and up to the time they were taken away, carriages, and vehicles were continually passing by the spot. No expressions of regret or pity are heard from any source.

SAN FRANCISCO (CA) CALL
January 19, 1901

COLORED MEN WAGE WAR AGAINST LYNCHERS. REWARD OFFERED FOR APPREHENSION OF MEN WHO BURNED FRED ALEXANDER.

SEATTLE, Jan., 18.—The Seattle branch of the International Council of the World, an organization of colored citizens, at a meeting held tonight in this city, decided to offer a reward of $500 for the apprehension and conviction of each and every person implicated in the death by violence of Fred Alexander, at Leavenworth, Kansas on Thursday night. Copies of the resolutions passed at the meeting will be forwarded to the Governor of Kansas, the Sheriff of Leavenworth County, and the Chief of Police of Leavenworth. The other councils throughout the country are asked to cooperate in the work.

WASHINGTON (D.C.) TIMES
February 28, 1901

TAKEN FROM JAIL AND HANGED FRO A MURDER. A WHITE MAN LYNCHED.

SCRANTON, MISS., Feb. 27.—The body of John Knox, a white man, is dangling from a tree here today. He was lynched for the murder of Don Davis by a mob made up of about 100 men last night. They were fully armed. they caught and bound the sheriff and his deputies, and battered down the jail door, soon securing their prisoner.

After Knox was hanged many shots were fired into his body. Knox made no protest on the way out of the jail, simply repeating the words, "I did not mean to do it." He was addicted to drink and killed Davis while drunk.

NEW YORK TIMES
March 17, 1901

TENNESSEE NEGRESS LYNCHED. WAS SUSPECTED OF FINDING AND KEEPING A PURSE CONTAINING $120.

NASHVILLE, Tennessee, March 16.—Ballie Crutchfield, a colored woman living near Rome, Smith County, was killed during the night by a mob, who took her from her cabin, carried her to a bridge, where she was bound, shot to death, and thrown into the creek. The woman was suspected of having found and failed to return a lost purse containing $120.

DESERET EVENING NEWS (GREAT SALT LAKE CITY, UT)
April 17, 1901

FATHER OF A LYNCHED NEGRO WANTS THEM ARRESTED.

LEAVENWORTH, Kan., April 16.—County Attorney Michael refuses to state what he will do regarding the issuing of warrants for the leaders of the mob that lynched Fred Alexander, the negro. The father of Alexander is emphatic in his demands for a warrant for W.G. Forbes, father of the girl assaulted, and who touched off the fire at the stake. A.M. Thomas, a negro lawyer, arrived here from Topeka today, and is said to be gathering evidence against the lynchers.

SALT LAKE (UTAH) TRIBUNE
April 9, 1901

$2000 INDEMNITY PAID TO MEXICAN CITIZEN.

WASHINGTON, April 8.—The Mexican Ambassador today received from the Secretary of State a draft for $2000, paid out of humane consideration and without reference to the question of liability, as full indemnity to the heir of Florentino Suaste, a Mexican citizen, who was lynched in La Salle County, Texas, in 1895.

WASHINGTON POST
May 19, 1901

$5000 LYNCHING INDEMNITY AWARDED.

The Ohio Supreme Court has decided that the taxpayers of one of the counties must pay $5,000 to the relatives of a negro who was lynched for a most heinous crime. This appears to be rather hard on those who didn't participate in the lynching.

WEEKLY TALLAHASSEEAN (FLORIDA)
June 6, 1901

ENGLISH IDEAS OF LYNCHING.

At a recent dinner in London the conversation turned on the subject of lynchings in the United States. It was the general opinion that a rope was the chief end of man in America. Finally the hostess turned to an American, who had taken no part in the conversation and said:

"You sir, must have often seen these affairs."

"Yes," he replied, "we take a kind of municipal pride in seeing which city can show the greatest number of lynchings yearly."

'Oh, do tell us about a lynching you have seen yourself,' broke in half a dozen voices at once.

"The night before I sailed for England," said the American, "I was giving a dinner to a party of intimate friends when a colored waiter spilled a plate of soup over the gown of a lady at an adjoining table. The gown was utterly ruined, and the gentlemen of her party at once seized the waiter, tied a rope around his neck, and, at a signal from the injured lady, swung him into the air."

'Horrible!' said the hostess, with a shudder. 'And did you actually see this yourself?'

"Well, no," said the American apologetically. "Just at that time I was down stairs killing the chef for putting mustard in the blancmange."—*Modern Society.*

VALENTINE (NEBRASKA) DEMOCRAT
June 30, 1901

NEGROES ARE ARMING.

LEAVENWORTH, Kan., June 17.—Considerable excitement has been caused by what appears to be a scheme of the negroes at Leavenworth to arm themselves with revolvers purchased from soldiers at Fort Leavenworth. Every since the burning of Fred Alexander, the negroes of Leavenworth have been in an ugly mood. And, conservative men say that the race feeling stirred up at that time may break out any time.

NEBRASKA STATE JOURNAL (LINCOLN, NE)

August 11, 1901

THE APPLAUSE FOR SENATOR TILLMAN.

[*WASHINGTON POST.*]

And so Senator Tillman has been applauded by a Wisconsin audience because he defended lynching in South Carolina. Will wonders never cease? Human nature is the same everywhere. In this country especially there is an enlightened regard for women, and a desire to shield her from all harm. Despite the occasional episodes of the divorce court, the sacredness of the marriage tie is a national characteristic, and love for family a universal. Upon the broad platform of esteem for women the people of Wisconsin and South Carolina stand shoulder to shoulder. Senator Tillman, therefore, appealed to every chivalrous instinct when he asserted that the summary execution of negroes who assault white women prevented the appearance of the latter in a public court to testify to their degradation in the presence of a mixed throng.

This argument could be easily understood. It was an abstract proposition. It went right to the narrow of the situation. Probably the first time in their lives, these Wisconsin people looked at lynching from the standpoint of a southern man, and putting themselves in his place, they manifested their sympathy and approval by applause. They now understand why prompt retribution is visited upon bestial negroes in Ohio as well as South Carolina.

Lynching is undoubtedly to be condemned. It is at odds with law, and with everything that goes to make good order in society. At the same time, how is Senator Tillman's argument to be answered? Shall the unhappy victim of a brutal assault give her evidence in secret? If there is to be any trial at all, all the forms of law must be observed. The grand jury must listen to the revolting details, and when an indictment has been found the woman must repeat the examinations and cross-examinations, exceptions and appeals, and all the other trickeries and resources of legal method. Anything less than this would be a mistrial, and a mockery, and would be more to be regretted than no trial at all.

Senator Tillman ought not to be so blunt and practical in defense of lynching. He will disturb the minds of more people than the few hundreds who gathered in his Wisconsin audience.

RICHMOND (VIRGINIA) DISPATCH
August 20, 1901

DOUBLE LYNCHING IN MISSOURI.

PIERCE CITY, MO., August 19.—Will Godley, a negro, was lynched by a mob, composed of 1,000 armed citizens, shortly after dark tonight, for the murder of Miss Carelle Wild, whose dead body was found today in the woods near here. The mob went to the jail, about 9 o'clock, battered down the doors, and threw ropes around the necks of Godley and Gene Carter. Godley was hanged in front of the Lawrence Hotel, and his body riddled with bullets. Carter was later taken out by the mob, riddled with bullets, and left dying in the street.

MINNEAPOLIS (MN) JOURNAL
September 4, 1901

RELICS WERE PLENTY.

This has been a great day for the relic enthusiast. The old-timer brought many interesting mementos of early days with them. There was a belt and pipe which Hole-in-the-Day, the famous Chippewa Chief, had presented to one of the pioneers. The first cradle in St. Paul, called the Larpenteur cradle, made its regular annual appearance along with the Godfrey cradle, first rocked at St. Anthony within sound of the falls.

Edwin Clarke exhibited a chain brought in by one of the pioneers of Little Falls. This did duty during one of the first lynchings in Minnesota. Three Indians who had committed murder were strung up in '57 by a party, at the head of which was Anson Northrop. The chain was buried with the reds, and recovered only last year. This is its first appearance in public as a historical relic.

MANITOBA DAILY FREE PRESS (WINNIPEG, MANITOBA, CANADA)
September 13, 1901

NEGROES LYNCH NEGROES. THREE MURDERERS TAKEN FROM A KENTUCKY JAIL AND HANGED BY A MOB.

[From the Associated Press]

CAIRO, Ill., September 12. — A mob of negroes last night broke into the jail at Wickliffe, Ky., across the river from this city, and lynched three negroes, Frank Howard, Sam Reed, and Ernest Harrison. They hanged the men to a crossbeam in a mill. The crime for which the men were hanged was the murder of an old and respected negro whom they killed and robbed. The murderers confessed their crime before the mob.

SUBURBAN CITIZEN (WASHINGTON, D.C.)
October 12, 1901

WHITE MAN LYNCHED.

NASHVILLE, Tenn., (Special).—News reached Nashville of the lynching of a white man named Mathew Wilson, residing near Rutherford, a small town not far from Trenton, Tenn. Wilson was arrested on Saturday afternoon charged with having entered the home of his father-in-law a few nights ago with the intention of criminally assaulting his 16-year-old sister-in-law. He was also held on the charge of housebreaking. In both case he was bound over to court.

NEW YORK TIMES
October 25, 1901

NEGRO BURNED AT STAKE.

COLUMBIA, Miss., Oct. 24.—The negro Bill Morris, who attacked Mrs. John Ball at Balltown, La., was burned at the stake today. After being captured he made an effort to implicate others, but they proved their innocence. Morris was taken to the scene of his crime and chained to a pine sapling. His hands and feet were bound to his body. Pine knots and pine straw were piled about his body and saturated with coal oil, and the match applied. The negro made no resistance when being bound to the stake, and said he deserved his fate. Morris beat his victim on the head with a pine knot, and thought he had killed her.

Going back to Ball's store, he took all the change in the cash drawer. Then he put coal oil on his feet, and also on his tracks when leaving the store. Mrs. Ball, however, recovered consciousness, and crawled to her father-in-law's house. He at once gave the alarm and the neighborhood commenced a search for the negro. He was found at his home, about four miles from the scene of the tragedy, and in trying to escape was shot by one of the posse and wounded in the hip.

SHINER (TX) GAZETTE
December 11, 1901

AN UNUSUAL SCENE.

LITTLE ROCK, ARK., Dec. 7.—Bud Wilson, a convict, who killed R.H. Naylor, a guard of the Yell County convict camp, last September, was hanged yesterday at Danville. The trap was sprung at 9:45 o'clock, and at 10:05 the body was lowered into a coffin. Before the lid was placed upon the coffin the body began moving about. He opened his eyes and his whole frame shook with tremors. He was taken from the coffin by the deputies, and carried up to the steps to the scaffold for the purpose of hanging again. When the platform was reached the body became rigid, remaining so for a moment, and then became limp. Wilson was examined by the physicians, who finally pronounced him dead, death being caused by strangulation.

WEEKLY TALLAHASSEEAN (FLORIDA)
December 13, 1901

SENATOR HOAR FIGHTS LYNCH MOB.

SENATOR HOAR has introduced a bill giving the United States jurisdiction in cases of lynching, and making the crime punishable by death. Now let Hoar introduce a bill making the crime for which lynchings are committed punishable by death. There will be lynchings as long as these outrages are committed. The perpetrator may escape for a time, but the people will lynch him when they catch him, regardless of Hoar and his lynching bill.

NORFOLK (NE) WEEKLY NEWS JOURNAL
January 17, 1902

SHERIFF PREVENTS LYNCHING.

PRESCOTT, Ark., Jan 16.—Three negroes, who are charged with the killing of two white men, were brought here from the penitentiary at Little Rock, where they were confined for safe keeping, to appear before the grand jury. A mob attempted to lynch them, but was prevented from doing so by the sheriff and six deputies, who held the crowd at bay with Winchesters until they could board the train for Little Rock. The negroes have been returned to the penitentiary.

SCRANTON (PA) TRIBUNE
January 20, 1902

SIOUX INDIAN LYNCHED. STOLE HORSE WHILE ON HIS WAY HOME FROM THE DEADWOOD JAIL.

[By Exclusive Wire from the Associated Press.]

DEADWOOD, S.D., Jan. 19.—John Yellow Wolf, a Sioux Indian, who was released from the Deadwood Jail two weeks ago, was lynched for horse stealing while on the way to his home on the Rosebud Reservation. When Yellow Wolf started for the agency he had a worthless old horse and saddle. Below Rapid City he turned the old horse loose, and caught a young hors out of a pasture on which to complete the journey.

He was overtaken by a number of men, and later was found dangling to a tree near White river. Yellow Wolf had served several terms in the Deadwood jail for various offences.

THE (EARLINGTON, KY) BEE
February 13, 1902

NEGRO LYNCHED. OUTRAGED A YOUNG LADY AT NICHOLASVILLE.

NICHOLASVILLE, Ky., Feb. 6.—Tom Brown, the negro who ravished Miss Della Power, was lynched in the courthouse yard at 1 o'clock this afternoon. Brown was arrested by the officers, and followed by a mob of 200 men, and was taken to the residence of Miss Power. She positively identified him as her assailant, but begged the mob not to lynch him. The leaders replied that they would do so at all hazards, and she plead with them not to add to her anguish by hanging him near her house. The mob agreed to this and came back with the officers, their number increasing every minute.

When they reached here the mob, which had surrounded the officers, seized the negro, and strung him up in a tree. There was no effort at concealment of their identity on the part of anybody connected with the mob. The lynching was very quietly done.

CLAY CITY (KENTUCKY) TIMES
May 15, 1902

GRUESOME STATISTICS.

THE *Chicago Tribune*, which keeps account, so far as it can, of murders, hangings, and lynchings in this country, reports that, in 1901 there were 118 legal executions—one less than in 1900. It reports for the year 135 lynchings (20 more than in 1900), of which 121 occurred in the south and 14 in the North, as compared with 107 in the South and 8 in the North in 1900.

The number of negroes lynched last year was 107, the same number as 1900. Of these, 39 were lynched for murder, the same number as in 1900, and 19 for criminal assault, as against 18 in 1900. There were fewer lynchings last year in Mississippi, Louisiana, and Georgia, but more in Alabama, Tennessee, and Texas. These figures bring out one fact that should be notice at least once a year. The number of negroes lynched every year for murder is more than twice as

---

HONOLULU (HAWAII) INDEPENDENT

May 27, 1902

EDITORIAL COMMENTARY: THE AMERICAN CIVILIZERS & LYNCHING.

How would it do to recall some of the military civilizers who are so sternly stamping out outlawry among the little brown folk on the other side of the Pacific, and set them to work at a similar task among white lynching mobs at home? While the Americans are busily engaged engrafting their ideas of higher civilization at the point of the bayonet, and with the help of the "water cure," mob law flourishes in Mississippi, Texas, and others of the Southern States.

Since the Filipinos are represented as close students of American newspaper literature, isn't it just possible that their objection to being "assimilated" arises from failure to appreciate this peculiarly American article of progress and culture?

HIGHLANDER RECORDER (MONTEREY, VA)

May 30, 1902

NEGRO TORTURED TO DEATH.

DALLAS, Texas, (Special).—Dudley Morgan, a negro was burned at the stake near Hallsville, 100 miles east of Dallas, for assaulting Mrs. McKee, a white woman, the wife of a section foreman of the Texas and Pacific Railway. Morgan was captured near Mount Pleasant and identified. After being bound he made this statement: "Tell my wife good-bye and tell her how I went. Tell her I was guilty of the charge, and it all occurred on account of Whaley Hurd. He persuaded me to do it, and said he would do the same thing. We planned it at the section-house before day Saturday."

WASHINGTON TIMES
June 7, 1902

MOB'S CURIOUS PRANK.

COLUMBIA, S.C., June 6.—A mob did a curious thing last night after the lynching of Jim Black, at New Road yesterday, for the murder of Mrs. Jones. The mob proceeded to Walterboro, forty miles away, where Cain Ford, implicated by Black, was in jail. Three deputy sheriffs were overpowered and sacks tied over their heads. One fired into the thicket of the crowd, but nothing is known of the result. Ford was taken away. It was believed everywhere that he had been lynched. This afternoon he was found tied to a tree, alive, and unhurt, a mile from Walterboro, and is again in jail.

COLORED AMERICAN (WASHINGTON, D.C.)
July 19, 1902

"POCKET BOOK CURE" FOR LYNCHING.

Touch the pocket nerve of the taxpayers in every county, city, town, or village in which a lynching occurs, and within a reasonable time the courts would be permitted in every part of the United States to deal with criminals in proper and orderly ways. If every state would pass a law imposing an extremely heavy fine upon any community in which the offence of lynching was committed, and would enact effective measures for the collection of such fines, mob murders would be few and far between.—*New York Tribune.*

SCRANTON TRIBUNE
July 25, 1902

FIERCE RACE WAR IN WEST VIRGINIA.

[By Exclusive Wire from the Associated Press.]

PHILIPPI, W.Va.,—Two negroes, whose names were unknown, were lynched at Womelsdorf, near here, last night by an angry mob numbering several hundred, and their mutilated bodies left on the common. The first victim was shot and instantly killed in the station house, the second was taken to the park, where he was hanged and then riddled with bullets, and cut to pieces.

Both whites and negroes are enraged and in arms. More trouble is expected. The trouble grew out of the murder of Chief Bud Wilmoth, July 23. Several other arrests had been made and lynching seemed imminent on every side. The dead blacks were caught near Bollington, and were locked up there, officers fearing lynching if taken to Elkins. Negroes are leaving on every train.

THE PADUCAH SUN
August 1, 1902

NEGRO ACCUSED OF MURDERING A WHITE MAN IS EXECUTED.

WASHINGTON, August 1.—Charles Craven, the negro accused of murdering William H. Wilson, near Herndon, Va., and who was captured this morning and taken to Leesburg, Va., was lynched this afternoon.

Craven, who has been pursued by over 100 people and bloodhounds, was captured today on a farm near Ashburn, Va. He was asleep in a hayrack, and was seized by three of his pursuers before he had time to offer resistance.

THE NEW YORK EVENING WORLD
August 14, 1902

LYNCHED INNOCENT MEN.

PARSONS, W.Va., Aug. 14.—Henry Lancaster, the negro in jail here in connection with the murder of Chief of Police F.H. Wilmot at Womelsdorf (Coalton), W.Va., now says that Clements and Carroll, the two negroes lynched, were the wrong men, and that the murderer was James Black.

COLORED AMERICAN (WASHINGTON, D.C.)
September 20, 1902

LITTLE COLORED AMERICANS.

Some white men who do not think with their minds accuse Negroes of shielding men of their color who are guilty of crime. Negroes do sometimes insist that their brethren be convicted of crime before being adjudged guilty, but as for covering up the misdeeds of their race, it is a well known and notorious fact that the majority of Negroes who are wanted by authorities are apprehended upon information formulated by Negroes familiar with the whereabouts of the alleged criminals.

HOUSTON (TEXAS) DAILY POST
November 17, 1902

MOB NOT SATISFIED WITH LIFE SENTENCE GIVEN. A WHITE MAN IS LYNCHED.

ELIZABETHTOWN, Ky., November 16.—Harlan Buckles, who was yesterday sentenced to life imprisonment for the murder of Robert L. Reid, was hanged by a mob shortly after 2 o'clock this morning.

The mob consisted of from 50 to 75 men, some of whom are supposed to have come from Larue County. On account of their number, they had little difficulty in getting Buckles from the jail. He was taken to the court house yard and hanged to a tree, after which the mob dispersed. Reid was deputy marshal here at the time he was killed.

Anti-Lynching Advocate, Mary Church Terrell. Terrell aspired to have a "lynch free" year in America.

John Jr. Mitchell, was the editor and anti-lynching advocate of the African American newspaper, *The Richmond (Virginia) Planet* for nearly 45 years, from 1884-1929.

WASHINGTON POST
January 15, 1903

MOB BAFFLED BY SUICIDE.

[Special to The *Washington Post*]

GREENWOOD, Miss., June 14.—A mob of more than 1,000 men, who attempted to capture and lynch Jim Williams, a negro, set fire to the house where he had barricaded himself today, and watched him shoot himself when the flames reached him. Williams killed the cook of a white family of Greenwood, and threw her baby out of a second-story window. He escaped and bloodhounds were placed on his trail. For more than 45 hours, through the Yazoo River swamps, the dogs followed the negroe's trail, finally leading the mob to a deserted cabin. When the mob charged the house, Williams fired upon the leaders, wounding two of them. Unable to get close enough to take him, the mob threw lighted torches at the cabin until it caught fire. Williams, finding escape impossible, fired a shot from his revolver into his brain. His charred body was found after the fire had been put out.

RICHMOND (VIRGINIA) DISPATCH
January 16, 1903

TEN WHITE MEN JAILED FOR LYNCHING NEGROES.

KOSCIUSKO, MISS., January 15.—Sheriff Love and posse brought in and lodged in jail today, ten white citizens of the northern part of this country, charged with the lynching of Jim Gaston and Monroe Hallum, two negroes, at the cross roads, last August. These men and a number of others have been indicted by the grand jury of Attala County. The names of the prisoners are A.E. Kierta, A.R. Tucker, Bill Goff, Bob Millner, Jim Green, John Green, Lee Whatley, Jim Whatley, Carlson Carlisle, and Oliver Wassen.

TIMES—DISPATCH (RICHMOND, VA)
February 8, 1903

LYNCHED THE NEGRO WHO KILLED SHERIFF.

WRIGHTSVILLE, Ga., Feb. 7.—Lee Hall (colored), who shot and mortally wounded Sheriff D.A. Crawford, of Johnson County, last Wednesday night, was taken from the county jail here today and lynched. Hall was captured yesterday, and was brought here and jailed yesterday afternoon. Threats were made early in the night, but later the excitement had somewhat subsided. Early this morning, however, a mob forced the jail officials to deliver Hall, whom they carried a few miles from Wrightsville and lynched. Sheriff Crawford is reported today to be barely alive.

NEW YORK SUN
April 16, 1903

INNOCENT NEGRO LYNCHED. WRONG MAN SHOT & BODY BURNED BY A MOB.

NEW ORLEANS, April 15.—It is now established beyond doubt that the negro killed near Shreveport by two police officers as the murderer of Mrs. Frank Matthews and her little daughter, and whose body was burned by a mob, was not, and could not have been the murderer. The lynched negro was reported to be Ed Porter. It turns out that he was really named Albert Washington, from the Vance plantation, in Bossier, who had come to Shreveport to find his wife, who had deserted him.

Washington was seen at the plantation at an hour that made it impossible for him to have committed the murder. And, in spite of the burning of the body, he was identified by a bag bearing his name found in his pocket, by other article in his clothes, and by his shoes. Cal Vance, upon whose plantation Washington worked, says that he was a good negro, in whom he had every confidence.

TIMES-DISPATCH (RICHMOND, VA)
May 21, 1903

THREE LYNCHED NEAR TAMPA. ONE WAS WHITE.

BARTOW, FLA., May 20.—Following the murder of Barney Brown, reported yesterday, 3 men were shot to death this morning, about daylight at Mulberry, a phosphate town eight miles west of Bartow.

The dead are: Amos Randall, white, Don Kennedy, and Henry Goulding, coloreds. The negroes were question before Justice Cain's Court concerning the death of Brown. Their professed ignorance of the crime was not believed, and they were taken out into the darkness by an armed crowd, which demanded the truth. Goulding then broke down and told how Amos Randall had followed Barney Brown down the road Monday night, and shot him through the head. There were probably 25 men in the mob that raided Randall's bar this morning, and perhaps 200 shot altogether were fired. The bodies of the three men were literally riddled with bullets. Randall returned fire, but so far as known Justice Cain's court concerning the death without effect. Sheriff Tillis took charge of the bodies, and had them buried. In all probability no arrests will be made. Fully half a carload of whisky was seized by the officers in Randall's store. Randall came to this country several years ago from Pennsylvania, from where it is said he had a wife and daughters.

THE COLORED AMERICAN (WASHINGTON, D.C.)
June 20, 1903

THESE THINGS WILL HAPPEN WITH LYNCHINGS.

The Greensville, Miss., blood suckers lynched a colored man during the last week, claiming that he attempted a criminal assault upon a well known young lady, which we believe to be a lie. If the truth was known in the case it would be learned that she was only his mistress, but by being caught in company with her the poor fellow had to die. Just because the colored live in the south he dies.—*The Progress.*

We had a case very similar to this case, which *The Progress* spoke of, in a little town in West Virginia, the other day, not very far from Washington. It was this in substance: The father of a young white lady about 19 years old had a young colored man arrested for criminal assault, and the young colored man was put in the calaboose. Later in the day, the young white lady went to the jail and asked the jailer for some letters, that she had written to the colored man. The jailer refused to give them up, saying that they would be needed in the trial. The young lady left the jail and went to a nearby bridge, and jumped off, committing suicide. The moral is plain.

NEW YORK SUN
June 26, 1903

LYNCHED FOR BREAKING AN ARM.

BRINKLEY, Ark., June 25.—Clarendon, a town 16 miles south of this city, was the scene of a lynching bee this morning at about 7 o'clock. Jack Harris, a negro, was hanged to the rafters of the porch to the American Cotton Company's office. About fifteen masked men composed the mob. No shots were fired.

On last Sunday night the negro assaulted his landlord, John Coburn, a white planter living 8 miles east of Clarendon, breaking one of his arms, and inflicting numerous other wounds. Coburn's wife ran to his assistance with a gun and the negro Harris took flight.

Coburn rebuked the negro for taking a mule form the stable and using it all day without permission. Harris was captured the day following the crime, and taken to the county jail at Clarendon. The Sheriff held the prisoner in the barn, but the mob took him from the guard.

RICHMOND TIMES—DISPATCH (RICHMOND, VA)
July 1, 1903

BLOOD HOUNDS AND MEN IN PURSUIT OF NEGRO.

NEW BRAUNFELS, TEXAS, June 30.—Armed men are tonight pursuing with bloodhound a negro who today attempted to assault and mortally wounded Mrs. Emil Gronie, wife of a farmer, who lives five miles southeast of this point. The negro appeared at the Gronie home and demanded money. Before the woman could reply he seized her and threw her to the floor. The negro was armed with a razor, with which he slashed his victim across the abdomen. Bloodhounds were secured from San Antonio and put on the trail of the negro. Mrs. Gronie is still alive, but is not expected to survive the night. There is every reason to believe that the negro will be lynched if caught.

WASHINGTON POST
July 4, 1903

WHITE AND BLACK LYNCHERS. JOHN OSBORNE HANGED BY A MIXED MOB AT CHARLOTTE, NC.

[Special to the *Washington Post*]

Charlotte, N. C. July 3.—John Osborne, a negro man, twenty-four years old, was taken from two deputy sheriffs early this morning by a mob of 200 men, composed of both whites and blacks, and strung up to a tree. The crime for which Osborne was lynched was committed in Union County Monday morning, at 2 o'clock.

His victim was Mrs. Lizzie Wentz, an aged and decrepit white woman, who lived in seclusion about twelve miles from this city. Osborne admitted his guilt, and said he deserved the punishment that was meted out to him. He was hanged to a tree limb, and left swinging. Gov. Aycock will send special officers to this section, in the hope that some of the mob may be brought under the law.

DESERET EVENING NEWS (GREAT SALT LAKE CITY, UT)
July 4, 1903

PREACHING THE JUSTIFICATION OF LYNCHING.

THE most disgraceful feature of the whole disgraceful lynching affair at Wilmington was the lynching sermon of the Rev. R.A. Ellwood, of the Olivet Presbyterian Church, of that city. That a minister of the gospel of Christ should be so lost to the meaning of his Master's teaching, and so forgetful of his responsibility for reckless utterances in the guise of religious instruction, as to apologize beforehand for burning the wretched murderer at the stake, and tell the mob that not they, but somebody else, would be morally responsible if they indulged in their passion for blood, almost passes understanding.

Not on the judges' head, where he sought to put it, but upon his own head, is the blood so barbarously shed by the populace who went out and did the killing which he urged upon them from a Christian pulpit.

CLAY CITY (KY) TIMES
July 9, 1903

STOP THE ASSAULTS

REV. G.C. Lorimer one of the most famous living divines, uttered this strong pulpit declaration as to lynching last Sunday: "Instead of holding meetings to denounce these lynchings, we should meet with a view of forever stopping these barbarous assaults on the women of our land. They are too frequent, and what wonder human nature boils over before such a bloody deed? We should make it plain that white men will not tolerate attacks upon their wives and daughters.

This is the imperative duty of the hour, and I trust it may not be overlooked by our colored citizens in their talk about social prejudice. Lynching is a regrettable affair, but the wanton murder of a defenseless woman is more so. This butchery of our woman must be blotted out." Dr. Lorimer strikes at the root of the lynching evil. Let the crime that leads up to the lynching cease, and lynching will be heard of no more. "This butchery of our women must be blotted out."—*Glasgow Times.*

NEW YORK TRIBUNE
July 16, 1903

WORK OF KENTUCKY MOB BY REASON OF LAW'S DELAY. A WHITE MAN LYNCHED.

MAYSVILLE, Ky., July 15.—Enraged at the tardiness of the courts, a mob broke into the Flemingsburg jail this morning and hanged William Thacker, a white man, to whom had been given a life sentence for the murder of John Gordon two years ago. Thacker, in a quarrel with Gordon at Foxport, shot and killed him and then sat on the body, Winchester in hand, while he smoke his pipe, and dared anyone to attempt to arrest him. At the time Thacker escaped, but was later arrested and lodged in jail at Flemingsburg. He had two trials and finally got a life sentence.

Gordon was a good citizen, and an inoffensive man. After being sentenced, Thacker appealed to the Court of Appeals, and was awaiting another trial. Thacker had some money, and was able to command the support of some influential men, and it was feared that he might escape punishment altogether.

The mob collected at Mount Carmel, where Gordon once lived, and came into Flemingsburg by twos and threes, in order not to arouse suspicion. They advanced upon the jail shortly after midnight. The jailer refused to surrender the keys. He was overpowered and the keys were taken away from him.

Thacker was hurried to a tree near the jail, and time was given him in which to say his prayers. He refused to do this, but begged for his life. To hush his cries, he was hit in the head with a rock, and his unconscious body strung up until life had become extinct.

SAN FRANCISCO (CA) CALL
July 18, 1903

LYNCHING REPORTS UNSEAT REASON.

KALISPELL, Montana, July 17.—Ed Burrill, a negro carpenter, has gone insane from reading reports of lynching of negroes in the South. He ran amuck last night, shouting out that a mob was after him to lynch him. He was taken to the State insane asylum today.

ATLANTA CONSTITUTION
July 19, 1903

NEGRO LYNCHED BY NEGRO POSSE. BODY LITERALLY SLASHED TO PIECES BY POCKET KNIVES. NO ARRESTS MADE.

JACKSONVILLE. Fla., July 18.—(Special.) A negro tramp by the name of Adams was lynched by negroes last night in Santa Fe swamp near Lake Butler. The negro had assaulted a colored woman by the name of Martha Jones, a few days previously. The crime was a most brutal one, and it is thought the woman will die.

Colored men in Bradford County gathered and hunted Adams down. Yesterday afternoon they found the negro in the Santa Fe swamp and lynched him. Not a white man was present, and the lynching was systematically conducted. There was no disorder whatsoever. While the body was swinging from a limb, many negroes pulled out their pocketknives and literally slashed the body to pieces.

Over one hundred cuts were shown on the body of the dead negro, which presented a horrible sight. Sheriff Johns, of Bradford County, has gone to the scene, but it is not thought that there will be any arrests. The coroner's inquest returned the customary verdict, came to death from the hands of parties unknown.

SAN FRANCISCO (CA) CALL
July 20, 1903

NEGRO MOB BREAKS INTO JAIL. VILLAGE MARSHAL PREVENTS LYNCHING OF A COLORED WOMEN'S ASSAILANT.

ST. LOUIS. July 19.—The jail at Brooklyn, a suburb of East St. Louis, across the river from here, was broken open tonight by a mob of negroes whose desire it was to lynch one of their own color for an attack upon a negress earlier in the day.

William Carter, the negro prisoner, was hurried from the jail by Village Marshal Speed, who took him in a roundabout way to St. Louis for safekeeping after the mob had broken open the door with a railroad tie. There was no other prisoner in the jail at the time.

WASHINGTON POST
July 27, 1903

LYNCHED A NEGRO WOMAN. MOB'S VICTIM ACCUSED OF HAVING POISONED YOUNG WHITE GIRL.

SHREVEPORT, La. July 26.—News reached Shreveport today that a negress, Jennie Steer, who administered poison in a glass of lemonade to Lizzie Dolan, the sixteen-year-old daughter of John Dolan, from the areas of which she died, was lynched by an infuriated mob about sundown last night. The lynching occurred on the Beard plantation, near where the crime -was committed. Jennie Steer was stubborn to the last, denying her crime. But the proof against .her was direct and conclusive.

It is said the negress fled from the Dolan house as soon as her crime was known. She was found crouching in a hayloft. The negress indignantly denied the crime. She was taken to the Dolan homestead and fully- identified.

The mob then took her to a near-by tree, placed a rope around her neck, and again asked. her to confess. She refused; however, and was strung up without making admissions. While the body was dangling in midair, several bullets were fired into it by enraged citizens.

The victim of poison was a beautiful young girl, who was not known to have an enemy in the world. She died in horrible, agony, which accentuated the rage of the mob.

PADUCAH (KENTUCKY) SUN
July 27, 1903

WOMAN SWUNG UP IN LOUISIANA. A WOMAN LYNCHED.

SHREVEPORT, La., July 27.—Jennie Steer, a negress, was lynched on the Beard plantation for the supposed crime of poisoning Lizzie Dolan, a beautiful white girl, who was given poison in a glass of lemonade, and died in terrible agony.

The negress was a servant at the house and protested her innocence to the last. She was not suspected at first. She is now suspected of other murders in this section.

She was strung up like a man to the nearest tree, and several bullets were fired into her body. It is said the negress is the first woman ever hanged in the state.

NEW YORK TRIBUNE
July 27, 1903

LYNCHED WRONG NEGRO. IMPARTIAL MOB MAN NOW LYNCH THE RIGHT ONE.

[By Telegraph to The *Tribune*]

ATLANTA, Ga., July 26.—The Liberty County mob which followed through seven counties a negro, supposed to be "Ed" Claus, who assaulted Miss Susie Johnson, a young white woman, near Darien Junction finally got their man. After capturing the negro, he was strung up to a tree and riddled with bullets, though the negro protested his innocence. It now appears that the mob got the wrong negro after all.

Now information has been received from Darien Junction, where the crime was committed, that Claus has been captured at a small station, and that officers have gone to get him. Claus was reared in the village where he is now held, and there can be doubt as to his being the man wanted for the crime, and, consequently, that an innocent man was put to death by the mob. There was great indignation against Claus, and if the citizens of Liberty County can get him, it is quite possible that he also will be lynched.

NORFOLK (NEBRASKA) WEEKLY NEWS-JOURNAL
July 31, 1903

UTAH HAS ADMIRABLE LYNCHING RECORD.

UTAH is one of the four states in which there has not been a lynching since 1885—and the only western state. Surely the state of the Mormons has some credit coming.

TITUSVILLE (PA) MORNING HERALD
August 1, 1903

GEORGIAN MOB LYNCHES THE WRONG NEGRO.

A Georgia mob lynched the wrong negro for an assault upon a white woman, but is on the trail of the real culprit, and proposes to make amends for the mistakes.—*Washington Post.*

THE CENTRAL RECORD (LANCASTER, KY)
August 21, 1903

GENERAL LEE ON LYNCHING.

Gen. Fitzhugh Lee, while in Kansas City a few days since, thus preached the gospel of lynching.

"I don't believe in lynching. Nobody believes in lynching. However, continued the general, there is one of the objects achieved by lynching that is seldom considered. If a man, say a negro, shall assault a woman, perhaps some very dear relative of yours, he has got to be killed or arrested. If this negro is arrested, after his crime is brought into the courtroom, with its jury, its lawyers, the woman, the one who has suffered it already, is the prosecuting witness. She must appear and, perhaps, under the cross-examination of lawyers, relate even details of the assault, thus subjecting her to humiliation to an extreme degree."

SAN FRANCISCO CALL
October 8, 1903

TRY TO LYNCH INNOCENT MAN. INEBRIATES HANG A SUSPECTED THIEF IN A LONELY SPOT.

[Special Dispatch to *The Call.*]

SEATTLE, Wash., Oct. 7.—From Unga Island the steamer Bertha brings the story of a drunken lynching bee that came near ending in a tragedy. Daniel Colville, a fisherman, was the victim of the outburst of passion.

At Unga is a saloon, presided over by a retired sea captain name Larson. One day recently, Colville and his companions entered the place and Colville's friends became intoxicated. Colville was the only sober man in the crowd. Captain Larson them missed $299 in bank notes, and suspicion fell on Colville. The rest of the crowd, being drunk and feeling themselves incapable of giving him a fair trial, eliminate the legal part of the proceeding and took him to a lonely spot, where they tied his hand behind him, and hoisted him from the ground. When he regained consciousness he found himself lying on the ground. One of his persecutors, fearful of taking the life of one who had been so summarily tried, had taken the responsibility of slipping away from his friends and cutting Colville down.

Colville could do nothing but walk back to the saloon and face his judges, and this he did. They gave him four hours to leave the island. As a result, Colville arrived in Seattle on the ship St. Paul.

SALT LAKE (UTAH) HERALD

October 11, 1903

WHITE MAN LYNCHED.

CHICAGO, Oct. 10.—A special to the *Record-Herald* from Starke, Fla., says: Samuel Williams, a young white man, was lynched at Lawtey, near here, last night by a mob of citizens who were search for Alta Williams, an elder brother, who is accused of maltreating two girls. Samuel Williams refused to divulge the whereabouts of his brother and was strung up by the mob.

NEW YORK TRIBUNE

November 29, 1903

A GOOD RECORD GONE. FIRST LYNCHING IN DORCHESTER COUNTY, S.C.

CHARLESTON, S.C., Nov. 28.—The first lynching in the history of Dorchester County occurred today. Last night John Fagle, a negro, about thirty years old, attempted to assault a young woman at her home near Ross Station on the Southern Railway, thirty-seven miles from here. He fled to the swamps. Bloodhounds were soon on the trail, and the negro was captured. After being carried before the woman and identified, he was strung to a tree limb, and his body riddled with bullets.

GAINESVILLE (FLORIDA) STAR

January 5, 1904

ALLEGED LYNCHERS ARRESTED.

Information from Pineapple, Alabama is to the effect that the sheriff of Wilcox County has arrested Walter Stuart, constable of Pineapple Precinct; Pressley Stuart, his brother; Evander Melton, uncle of “Pig” Melton; Robert Ray, a gypsy horse trader, and Emmett Barlow.

The trial will be held before Justice Crawford. Solicitor Quarles was telegraphed of the arrests.

NEW YORK TIMES
February 8, 1904

WOMAN AND MAN BURNED AT STAKE.

MEMPHIS, Tenn., Feb. 7.—Luther Helbert and his wife, colored, who murdered James Eastland, a young planter at Doddsville, Miss., Wednesday morning, were captured after a three days' chase in a swamp on the Yazoo River Sunday morning at 3 o'clock.

They were taken to Doddsville by a band of 50 men and were burned at the stake, near the scene of their crime, at 3:30 this afternoon, before a large crowd of men from three counties. The two brothers of the murdered planter decided the form of punishment and were present at the burning. The crime for which the negro died was one of the most horrible cold-blooded ever committed in this State.

The mob turned the sixteen-year-old son of the murderer loose. The boy had been force to accompany them. The negroes were heavily armed when captured, and were expected to make resistance, as they had sworn not to be taken alive. However, they were surprised when asleep in the swamp. Seven negroes, including the murderers and the negro who was killed in company with young Eastland, have suffered death as the result of this crime. It is thought that the negro lodges in that section had much to do with the crime, and that they helped the murderers.

THE BEE (EARLINGTON, KENTUCKY)
March 10, 1904

KENTUCKY NEGRO. LYNCHED BY OHIO MOB—BODY STRUNG UP IN STREET.

SPRINGFIELD, Ohio, March 7.—An enraged mob of nearly

1,000 men tonight battered down the doors of the jail and lynched Richard Dixon, of Cynthiana, Ky., a negro who shot and killed Patrolman Charles Collis yesterday. The jail was thought to be impregnable, but the infuriated mob used railroad irons on the heavy doors successfully. When inside, the Sheriff and his deputies surrendered in face of such superior force, and the negro was taken to the jail yard and shot to death. The body was then taken to the corner of Main Street and Fountain Avenue, and hanged to a telegraph pole. The mob then spent half an hour riddling it will bullets fired from several hundred revolvers.

NEW YORK TIMES
March 12, 1904

BOYS TRY TO LYNCH NEGRO. SPRINGFIELD CHILDREN EMULATE THEIR ELDERS, BUT THE VICTIM IS RESCUED.

SPRINGFIELD, Ohio, March 11.—The effect of lawlessness and rioting upon the minds of the "young idea" were illustrated tonight at the Shaffer Street school, when there came near being a lynching, with the white children for lynchers and a colored child as the victim. Two white boys caught a negro boy, placed a rope around his neck, and began to drag him along the ground. The negro was rescued before serious injury had been done.

Since the lynching of the negro Dixon last Monday night the city has been closely guarded by eighteen companies of State militia, but today all the companies of the Third Regiment, excepting two local companies have been removed. Besides these two companies, there are still seven companies of the Second Regiment on duty, and these will be retained here at least until Monday.

WASHINGTON POST
March 18, 1904

LEARNING BY EXAMPLE.

[From the *New York Tribune*.]

The white children in Ohio who were caught trying to hang a negro child were merely learning the lesson taught by their elders. They furnish a striking illustration of the demoralizing influence of lynching. Few children may be actually moved to kill others, but they all learn to set less value on human life, and pay less reverence to law from the contemplation of lawless deeds.

OCALA EVENING STAR

April 29, 1904

THIS WAS IN IOWA! HONEST OLD NEGRO TORTURED TO DEATH BY YOUNG WHITE MEN.

HAMBURG, Iowa, April 27.—John C. Goodlow, an honest old negro, is dead, as the result of a fiendish practical joke perpetuated by a number of young men a few nights ago. Nevertheless, a coroner's jury certified that death was due to "natural causes."

Goodlow came to his death as a result of tortures and torments at the hands of his white companions, who, as a joke, accused him of an imaginary crime. After tying him with ropes, and nailing his feet to a board, they covered him with wood and shavings, and placed a rag saturated with kerosene near his nose. They then poured over him a bucket of water, and pretended they were going to light it.

Just then the old man's cries suddenly ceased. The jokers realized that their fun had been carried too far. They removed the debris and began to untie the negro, when they discovered that he was dead. He was carried quietly away and dumped into a corncrib, where he was found the next day. Goodlow was 61 years old, and had lived here for 26 years. He always provided well for his family.

NEW YORK SUN

May 11, 1904

NEGRO MOB KILLS A MAN. PURSUED TWO

BROTHERS WHO WERE SAID TO HAVE MURDERED A COLORED WOMAN.

NEW ORLEANS, May 10.—A mob of 400 negroes at Ballentine, Miss., yesterday pursued the Bobo brothers, who were said to have killed a colored woman. The negroes surrounded the Bobo's and killed Rufus. Mack Bobo was arrested and placed in jail; the mob surrounded the jail and demanded the prisoner for the purpose of lynching him.

Notice of the mob's intention was given to Sheriff Johnson at Sardis, the county seat. He hastened to Ballentine, and with the assistance of three deputies succeeded in disarming the mob and taking the prisoner safely to the county jail at Sardis.

RACINE (WISCONSIN) DAILY JOURNAL

June 14, 1904

PRESS COMMENTARY. LYNCHED THE WRONG NEGRO.

Milwaukee Sentinel: Probably the mob that lynched the wrong negro in Mississippi the other day has squared matters by apologizing handsomely to the victim's relatives.

OSHKOSH (WISCONSIN) DAILY NORTHWESTERN

June 15, 1904

INNOCENT CASE OF MISTAKEN IDENTITY.

They lynched the wrong negro down in Mississippi the other day. But then, mistakes will occasionally happen even in the best-intentioned communities.

ALEXANDRIA (D.C.) GAZETTE

June 16, 1904

NEGROES LYNCH NEGRO.

A negro named Jonah Woods, who lived in Heard County, about 25 miles from La Grange, Georgia was lynched by other negroes yesterday. Woods was a deacon in his church, and it is said he discovered a number of negroes playing "craps" and threatened that he would report them to the grand jury. Afterward, the church was burned down, and two days later, while prowling in the fields, Woods was seized and strung up to a tree nearby.

NEW YORK TIMES
June 16, 1904

KENTUCKY NEGRESS LYNCHED. SO HEAVY THE ROPE BROKE & MOB SHOT HER DOWN AS SHE RAN.

LEBANON JUNCTION, KY., JUNE 15.—Mrs. Maria Thompson, colored, who last night killed John Irwin, a white farmer, was taken from jail today and hanged to a tree in the jail yard. She weighed 255 pound and the rope broke. As she ran away the mob fired a fusillade after her until she fell and was left for dead. Later officers removed her to a physician's office, where she died.

SEMI-WEEKLY INTERIOR JOURNAL (STANFORD, KY)
June 21, 1904

NEGROE WOMAN MARY THOMPSON IS STILL WITH US!

Mary Thompson, the negro woman who killed John Irvin near Belmont, and was subsequently shot by a mob, is now in jail at Shepherdsville and will probably recover. The action of the mob will be investigated by the grand jury.

HOPKINSVILLE KENTUCKIAN

June 21, 1904

STILL ALIVE. MOBBED NEGRESS WILL RECOVER FROM HER WOUNDS.

SHEPHERDSVILLE, KY., June 16.—Mary Thompson, the negress, who was mobbed and shot by citizens of Lebanon Junction, after she had murdered a farmer by cutting his head off with a razor, is in jail here. She imagines a mob is trying to get her, but is otherwise recovering from her wounds. The negroes threatened to burn Lebanon Junction tonight, but the citizens are prepared to resist and no trouble is expected.

ADAIR COUNTY NEWS (COLUMBIA, KY)

June 22, 1904

NEGRO WOMAN SURVIVES LYNCHING.

A mob attempted to lynch a negro woman, Mary Thompson, at Lebanon Junction last Wednesday night. While she was hanging from a limb, she jerked a knife from the hand of one of the mob, cut herself loose, and fought her way from the crowd. In escaping, she was shot three times, but will probably recover. She is now in jail at Shepherdsville, and the negroes of Lebanon Junction threaten to burn the town where the attempted lynching occurred. The negro woman murdered a respectable white man the day before.

NEW YORK TRIBUNE

June 27, 1904

GIRL LYNCHES NEGRO. HE HAD ASSAULTED HER. SHE PUT NOOSE ON HIS NECK & LED HORSE FROM UNDER HIM.

EUPORA, Mississippi, June 26.—Starling Dunham, a negro, wanted on the charge of criminally assaulting the 16-year-old daughter of John Wilson, a white man, near Bellefontaine two weeks ago, and attempting to assault three young girls named Dunn near this city on the same day, was hanged in the public squared here today by a mob. The noose was placed about the negro's neck by the Wilson girl, who positively identified him as her assailant. The negro was then placed on the back of a large black horse. And, at a signal from the leader of the mob, the Wilson girl led the horse from under him. More than 3,000 persons, white and black, witnessed the execution. After being assured that the negro was dead, the mob cut down the body and turned it over to relatives for burial.

Dunham was captured on Friday near Vienna, Alabama, after a running chase, in which he was wounded in two places. He was brought here last night by the Sheriff of this county. A large mob met the train at the station, and an effort was made to get the negro, but the officers spirited him away and carried him to the jail at Waltham, six miles from here. In Waltham, he was again met by a mob, who said that their intention was to burn him. The officers succeeded in prevailing on the mob to give up this intention, but only after promising to give up the negro this morning for execution.

There was a strong sentiment for burning, but this was overcome, and the lynching took the form of a hanging. Dunham stoutly maintained his innocence to the last, and denied that he had ever seen the Wilson girl. He admitted having visited Dunn's place, but denied any bad motive. His last remarks were made to 200 negroes who were assembled about the point of execution. Dunham told them to never go around a white man's house when women were at home alone. The three Dunn sisters, the eldest of whom is less than 18-years-old, witnessed the lynching from a distance.

NEW YORK TIMES
August 23, 1904

REWARD FOR LYNCHERS.

MONTGOMERY, Ala., Aug. 22.—Acting Governor Cunningham today offered rewards for members of the mobs which have participated in three recent lynchings in the State, $150 for the first conviction in each case, and $100 for the next two. These cases are the lynchings of Will Roberts, July 6, in Pickens County; Rufus Lessuere, Aug. 16, in Marengo County, and that of Will Avery last Saturday at Cordova. He said:

"I expect to use every particle of power the laws of the State give me to prevent lynchings, and to punish those who take part in thc illcgal cxccution of men, white or black, charged with crimes.

ADAIR COUNTY NEWS (COLUMBIA, KY)
August 24, 1904

REED AND CATO LYNCHED.

Paul Reed and Will Cato, two negro men, were burned to death at a stake in Statesboro, Ga., last Wednesday. They were charged with murdering a white family. consisting of Mr. and Mrs. Hodges and their three children. Reed confessed, but Cato claimed that he was innocent. Reed said just before the torch was applied, that Henry Bell murdered the children, and that he was the murderer of the parents. It was a horrible crime, but the law could have been vindicated without inflicting inhuman punishment.

THE VICTIM OF THE MOB.

Will Reed and Ed Cato, Who were Burned to Death for Their Atrocious Crime.

THE STAKE AFTER THE HOLOCAUST.
Gruesome Relics of Mortality Strewed the Ground When the Mob Had Completed Its Fearful Work.

THE STAKE AFTER THE HOLOCAUST.

Gruesome Relics of Mortality Strewed the Ground When the Mob Had Completed Its Fearful Work.

SAINT PAUL (MN) GLOBE

September 7, 1904

CUT OFF NEGRO'S EARS AND LYNCH HIM.

BRUNSON, Fla., Sept. 6.—Wash Bradley the confessed negro murders of Mrs. N.B. Barrow, was today strung up to a tree and his body riddled with bullets after his ears had been severed from his head and his body otherwise mutilated.

Bradley's capture was made yesterday by Shed and Walter Howard, two negroes, at the home of another negro, after which he was turned over to the neighbors of the settlement. Bradley stated that he went to the residence for the express purpose of assaulting a daughter of Mrs. Barrow. When Mrs. Barrow was shot, she held a suckling babe at her breast. It escaped injury.

ATLANTA CONSTITUTION

September 9, 1904

WRONG NEGRO WAS CREMATED. AWFUL MISTAKE IS CHARGED TO MISSISSIPPI MOB.

JACKSON, Miss. September 8.—(Special.) —Was the real Starling Dunham, who committed the rape in Webster County, lynched and burned at the stake at Eupora last June? This is the question that is worrying the city police.

There is a negro in the Jackson jail, who says that his name is Starling Dunham, and officers here are convinced that the wrong negro was lynched at Eupora. The negro was arrested for vagrancy and gave his name as Smith. His actions aroused the suspicions of the officers and this afternoon they carefully examined the negro, and he tallied exactly with the description of Starling Dunham.

Then the negro became excited, and said his real name was Dunham, that he was wanted in Webster County for rape, but did not want to go back until he had the protection of a company of soldiers. The matter was laid before Governor Vardaman, and if he proved to be the real Dunham, he will be given protection if carried back.

COLORED AMERICAN
September 10, 1904

A TYPE OF THE "RESPECTABLE" GEORGIA CITIZEN.

Our cartoonist presents the readers of THE COLORED AMERICAN with a mild picture of the so-called "respectable" citizen of Georgia, better known as the "cracker." Not satisfied with lynching and burning colored people in their own State, the Georgia Militia is carrying on its work on its way North, en-route to Manassas. These same Militiamen, who were cowardly enough to permit a mob to take their guns away from them, are now engaged in their favorite "chivalrous" past time of stoning helpless colored women and men, and yet we are sending missionaries to other countries to Christianize and civilize the heathen.

COLORED AMERICAN **(WASHINGTON, D.C.) September 10, 1904:**
“A TYPE OF THE "RESPECTABLE" GEORGIA CITIZEN.”

PADUCAH (KY) SUN
September 28, 1904

WHY LYNCHING IS NOT STOPPED IN THE SOUTHERN STATES.

Huntsville, Ala., Sept. 28.—Ben Hill, the third alleged lyncher to be placed on trial, was acquitted. The jury spent two hours on the case and reported a verdict of not guilty. The state was unable to prove that Hill took an active part in the lynching of Horace Maples, as several witnesses testified that he was only a spectator.

PALESTINE DAILY HERALD
December 8, 1904

NEARLY LYNCHED. MURDERED WIFE'S GRANDMOTHER & THREW BODY IN FLAMES.

ATLANTA, Ga., Dec. 9.—A *Constitution* special from Columbus, Ga., says: Only the most determined effort on the part of white men has prevented the lynching of William Vaughn at the hands of a negro mob in Russell County, Alabama. Vaughn confessed that he robbed his wife's grandmother, set fire to her house, murdered her, and threw her bleeding body into the flames a few days ago. After the capture of Vaughn a mob of negroes quickly assembled. They were wrought up to a high pitch of excitement and threatened to deal out summary justice.

LOGANSPORT DAILY JOURNAL
January 5, 1905

THE VIGILANTS. SPENCER COUNTY DETERMINED TO BE RID OF VICIOUS CHARACTERS-WHITES SAME AS BLACKS.

EVANSVILLE, Indiana, January 4.—It is learned here today that a Vigilance Committee has been formed in Spencer County, since the recent lynching of three negroes, for the purpose of ridding the community of the vicious negroes and whites. The committee meets every Monday night at different places in order to divert suspicion from its acts. At each meeting, a notice is drawn up and served on one or more of the bad characters in the community to "Move on."

Since the first meeting was held, more than a dozen negroes have had notice to leave. Their records have been hunted up and given to them as a reason for the action of the committee. There is no parleying, and the action of the committee has not once been questioned. A system of detective work has been devised, and it is said to be working thoroughly and consistently with the desires of the committee.

The Vigilance Committee is composed of prominent men in the community, among whom are both Republicans and Democrats. After the vicious negro element is removed, attention will be turned to the whites who have notorious reputations. As a result of the work of the committee, it is said that the morals of the community were never better than since the vigilants began their work.

EVENING WORLD (NEW YORK, N.Y.)
January 3, 1905

NEGRO BOY LYNCHED.

HOPE, Ark., Jan 3.—As the result of an assault made by two negroes on a farmer named Nobbs, near Spring Hill, ten miles south of Hope, one of the negroes, White Jetton, has been taken from Constable Nelson Garner and lynched. A vigorous, but van search was made for Jetton's companion by the mob. Jetton is said to have been less than eighteen years old.

PADUCAH (KENTUCKY) SUN
June 26, 1905

500 SHOTS FIRED INTO "NEGRO HILL." 2 NEGROES SHOT.

CHATTANOOGA, Tenn., June 26.—As a result of bad blood between union and non-union miners at Whitwell, two negroes were shot by alleged union miners, and over 500 shots fired into the section of town known as "Negro Hill."

OCALA (FLORIDA) BANNER

September 15, 1905

WHITE MEN BURN A NEGRO.

JACKSON, Miss., Sept. 14.—Governor Vardaman has received a letter from District Attorney Brewer, of the eleventh district, notifying him that a negro boy, named Will James, living in the interior of Tallahatchie County, was taken to the woods by three white men and shot to death, after which his body was burned. The negro, it seems, had brought whisky form one of the white men, and afterwards informed on him. The district attorney asked the governor to take action in the case.

OCALA (FLORIDA) BANNER

September 15, 1905

SHERIFF PREVENTED A LYNCHING.

WINCHESTER, Ky., Sept 14.—Prompt action by Sheriff McCord probably saved Sam Hisle from lynching here today. Hisle, who had been held at Lexington since his arrest on a charge of assaulting Mrs. Marry Case, was brought here during the night for examination today. When news of his coming was received, a mob quickly formed and surrounded the jail. After arming his deputies and leaving them in charge of the prisoner, who was shrieking for mercy, Sheriff McCord walked alone and unarmed into the midst of the mob, and told them plainly that his men were armed and would shoot, and that they should let the law take its course.

LOS ANGELES (CALIFORNIA) HERALD

October 8, 1905

TEXAS CITIZENS WANT MOB LAW TO RULE.

By Associated Press.

CHICAGO, Ill., Oct. 7.—A dispatch to the Tribune from Houston, Texas, says:

A petition from a number of citizens headed by G.W. Knight, of San Marcos, has been presented to Governor Lanham, asking that the state permit mob punishment of negroes who assault women.

The governor is asked to indorse a policy of absolute non-protection to negroes guilty of assault, insuring that they be given no trial by legal inquiry of any kind, but that they be hanged instantly as soon as apprehended. Governor Lanham's response is principally directed to the legal phase of the proposition. He explains that it is impossible for him to countenance the policy in view of his oath of office and the state legislation, which he is bound to protect.

LOS ANGELES (CALIFORNIA) HERALD
November 13, 1905

BODIES OF LYNCHED NEGROES ARE CUT DOWN AND CLAIMED BY RELATIVES.

[By Associated Press.]
HENDERSON, Texas, Nov. 12.—All has been quiet here since the lynching of the three negroes this morning. The bodies of the victims were cut down shortly after the hanging, and have been claimed by relatives. After the men were hung the mob quietly dispersed. None of those who participated have been identified. The crime of which the negroes were charge was having killed Elias Howell, a white farmer.

NEW YORK TRIBUNE
February 12, 1906

FOUR MEN LYNCH NEGRO. BREAK INTO JAIL AND HANG ASSAULTER FROM RAILROAD BRIDGE.

GADSDEN, Ala., Feb. 11.—"Bunk" Richardson, a negro, charged with the assault and murder of Mrs. Sarah Smith here last July, was taken from jail at an early hour this morning and hanged to the bridge of the Louisville and Nashville Railroad, across the Coosa River.

Four masked men went to the jail, overpowered the sheriff and jailer, and made short work of the prisoner. Four negroes were charged with the crime against Mrs. Smith, two of whom have been legally executed. The third, Will Johnson, was recently convicted and sentenced to death, but last week Governor Jelks commuted the sentence to life imprisonment. Richardson, the man lynched this morning, had been indicted, but was in jail awaiting the action of the grand jury.

NEW YORK TRIBUNE
March 18, 1906

NEGRO LYNCHED FOR KILLING A COW.

For the crime of killing a white man's cow, William Carr, a Negro, was killed at Plaquemines, Louisiana. The lynching was conducted in a most orderly manner, Carr being taken from the Sheriff without resistance by a mob of thirty masked men, hurried to the nearest railroad bridge, and hanged without ceremony.

CHATTANOOGA (TN) TIMES
March 20, 1906

"GOD BLESS YOU ALL—I AM INNOCENT"

Protesting his innocence to the last and with the words "God bless you all" on his lips, Ed Johnson, the negro convicted of assaulting Miss Nevada Taylor in St. Elmo on the night of Jan. 23 was shot to death on the county bridge last night. The awful penalty was meted out by a small but determined band of men who stated that the courts had been given all the time due them and that they had made up their minds to take the law into their own hands.

Johnson's life was ended just as the court house clock struck 11. At 7 o'clock the negro was resting calmly in his cell happy over an official order from the United States Supreme Court which gave him an indefinite time to live. At the same hour the city was quiet and there was but little talk or thought of trouble. A half hour later there were rumors that a few men were getting together to lynch the negro, but nobody seemed to take the report seriously. An hour later the jail was invested, and disinterested spectators who had seen lynch law carried out before knew that the negro had only a short time to live.

At 8 o'clock a dozen men, a few with handkerchiefs over the lower part of their faces and the rest undisguised in any manner, walked into the jail office. A few minutes later another half dozen men came. Close upon the heels of these a few more strolled in. In all there were only about twenty-five, but each man seemed to know just what to do and the twenty-five did the work as efficiently as it could have been done by hundreds.

When the mob reached the jail only jailer Gibson was on duty. The leaders made demand upon on him for the keys. The jailer refused to yield and tried to argue with the men while he made a play for time. While the argument for the keys was going on a few of the men ran up the stairs to the corridor where Johnson was confined and one of them attempted to break the lock with a hammer. The attempt was only partially successful and delayed the mob more than anything they could have done. Meanwhile the men below had secured the keys from Jailer Gibson. They rushed upstairs and tired to turn the bold but the sledge hammer had made the keys useless.

Then began the work of battering the two heavy doors down. Man after man took his turn with the hammer and axe and rivet after rivet was knocked out. Men streaming with perspiration yielded their implements to others as their strength gave out and the work went on steadily. At 10:30 the first of the two doors was torn out, and the workers began on the second. It took only about five minutes to batter and pry the second door open and then the way to the Negro was clear.

The systematic manner in which the mod it its work was shown by the fact that when the doors were broken open only a half dozen men entered the corridor. One of these had the key to cell No. 7 the one in which Johnson was confined and he opened the door slowly and carefully and his helpers in the corridor seized the Negro and bound him with a rope which one of them carried and the doomed man was led outside and down the stairs.

As Johnson was brought out of the corridor and to the head of the stairs there was a cheer from the crowd awaiting him. About half of this crowd was made up of idle spectators who had done no work at all. Some of these became wildly excited at sight of the Negro and some of them began howling "Kill him now!" The men from the section where the crime was committed, however, had no intention of permitting a shooting in the jail. "To the county bridge," was the command of the leaders and to the county bridge the march was taken up.

Almost as dramatic as the lynching itself was that walk out Walnut street to the bridge. The men who had taken Johnson from the jail and meant to take his life were around him in a group. They had but little to say and they made no noise. Surrounding them was an excited mob or seventy-five or more who yelled at the top of their voices and pushed each other from one side of the street to the other.

When the bridge was reached it seemed the intention of the leaders to swing the unfortunate negro to the first span.

"The second span!" yelled the mob, and with this demand the leaders complied. When the place chosen was reached two men scrambled up the ironwork and pulled the rope, one end of which was around Johnson's neck, over the beam. The negro was then given a chance to talk and he was urged to make a confession. To all questions and demands for a confession he would only say, "I'm ready to die, but I never done it."

Finally it was decided that time was being wasted, and the order to hoist up the negro was given. Eager hands began to pull, but the rope slipped and more time had to be spent in adjusting it. When the hoisting finally began, the now frenzied lynchers could restrain themselves no longer, and a fusillade of shots was turned loose. One of the first bullets cut the rope and the body came tumbling to the bridge floor. Then the frenzied men from the suburban district, every one of whom had a gun or pistol, gathered around and emptied the contents of their weapons into the prostrate negro.

When all the firearms had been discharged the Negro was seen to move his head slightly. "He's not dead!" yelled men close to him, and this was followed up with demands for another gun. Then a big, broad-shouldered man, who had done much of the work, slowly refilled the chambers of his revolver. When his weapon was loaded to his satisfaction, he walked up to the Negro, stood directly over the body and fired five shots into it. This ended the work of the lynchers and they left the bridge so rapidly that the idly curious hardly knew they were going.

Dr. Cooper Holtzclaw reached the bridge a few minutes after the lynching. He said the Negro had been shot fifty times, and any one of the shots was sufficient to produce death. The body lay on the bridge for about an hour. Chapman finally sending a wagon for it.

RICHMOND (VA) TIMES-DISPATCH
April 26, 1906

17-YEAR-OLD NEGRO BOY LYNCHED.

OAKWOODS, TEX., April. 25.—A seventeen-year-old negro boy was lynched today by a mob of seven men, who took him from the custody of the officers. The negro had entered the home of a widow near town. He was caught and fully identified, and was awaiting transportation to the county seat. The deputy sheriff, who had the prisoner in charge, fired several shots at the members of the mob, but without effect.

NEW YORK TIMES
May 16, 1906

NEGRO SOLDIERS FIGHT MOB. KILLING TWO BENT ON LYNCHING ONE OF THEIR COMRADES.

[Special to the New York Times]
CRAWFORD, Nebraska, May 15.—In a fight which occurred here last night between a mob bent on lynching Sergeant Reed, the negro soldier who Sunday shot Marshal Moss through the heart, and negro soldiers who were guarding the jail in which Reed was

imprisoned, Phillip Murphy, alleged leader of the mob, and an unidentified man were killed by the soldiers.

Feeling is very bitter against the negro soldiers and serious trouble may break out at any time. The soldiers are from Fort Robinson, three miles away. Already four men have been killed in the troubles since Sunday afternoon. After the mob last night was dispersed by the soldiers, Reed was taken to Chadron on a special locomotive for safekeeping.

SALT LAKE CITY (UTAH) HERALD

May 30, 1906

BIZARRE OCCURRENCE—A WHITE MAN LYNCHED.

MONROE, La., May 29.—A mob of took a special train here last night. and went to Tallulah, La., where they forced their way in, and hanged R.L. Rogers, a white man. Rogers was the alleged murderer of Jesse Brown, a prominent merchant of Girard, La., Brown was killed Feb. 19, 1904

Rogers was tried and found guilty. He got a change of venue, and a mistrial was ordered. He was discharged on a plea of former jeopardy.

RICHMOND (VA) TIMES-DISPATCH

August 8, 1906

DAY OF EXCITEMENT CORPSES OF LYNCHED NEGROES MUTILATED FOR SOUVENIRS.

SALISBURY, N.C., August 7.—Today has been one of excitement in Salisbury, due to the events following the taking of the six Lyerly murderers from the jail last night by an overwhelming mob of 3,000, and lynching three of them, Nease Gillespie, John Gillespie, and Jack Dillingham.

At the earnest appeal of some level heads in the mob Delia Dillingham, Henry Gillespie, and George Irvin, concerning whom there was some doubt of their guilt, were turned over to a posse of deputies, who hustled them away in the darkness to an unused county building for safety.

It was at first reported that all had been lynched, and that the latter three had been burned. They were, however, today spirited away by officers to Charlotte, but before leaving were taken to the spot where the three lifeless bodies of their cellmates were dangling in the air with hundreds of bullet holes, expose to view.

Eyewitnesses to the lynchings state that Nease Gillespie and Jack Dillingham, who have at all times been considered the leaders of the gang of murderers, quarreled outright while the death rope was being place around their necks as they gazed at the huge limb which was to hold their bodies.

"You are to blame for all this," said Nease to Jack. The latter replied that Nease was the cause of the calamity, who in turned blamed Delia Dillingham with the entire affair.

At a very early hour this morning, Misses Maggie and Addie Lyerly, the only surviving members of the murdered family, were driven to the scene of the lynching and viewed with awe the three bodies swinging to a limb. The little girls have borne up thus far, and it is believed they will survive the shock, which at one time, was life threatening.

The Rowan jail was a versatile wreck this morning, with the exception of the three-story brick walls. Not only had every windowpane been broken, but the blinds and sash as well as doors had been literally thrashed to splinters by the fury of the mob, which used bricks and stones with telling effect.

The first entrance to the prison was effected by the leaders of the mob, chopping down the large rear doors. After gaining the stairway the locks to the cells were soon battered off and the prisoners taken. In the melee Ed Taylor, a white prisoner, and Tom Brow (colored), charged with burglary, escaped from the prison. The latter returned an hour afterward, begging for protection.

Following the lynching of the three negroes, thousands of people visited the scene. Many visitors, desirous of souvenirs, cut off fingers, ears and other parts from the dead bodies and carried the same away.

SAN FRANCISCO CALL
August 8, 1906

BODIES OF NEGROES MUTILATED. RELIC HUNTERS CUT OFF FINGER'S OF THE MOB'S VICTIMS FOR SOUVENIRS.

CHARLOTTE, N.C. Aug. 7.—Tonight three companies of the North Carolina National Guard surround the jail at Salisbury, while sent rich, with loaded guns and orders to shoot to kill, patrol the four streets that flank the prison. There have been threat and rumors of threats all day and night, but there has been no demonstration and it is believed the worst is over.

George Hall, the ex-convict from Montgomery County, who is said to have led the mob, which lynched the three alleged murderers of the Lyarly family last night, is in jail. The plan to rescue him, rumors of which caused Governor Glinn to hurry troops to Salisbury, has not materialized. The surviving negroes, Henry Lee, George Ervis, and two women, are safe in the jail at Charlotte, and there is no danger of violence to them.

Long before the moon rose, curious persons went to the scene of the lynching and cut off the toes, fingers, and ears of the negroes, who were hung to the limb of a tree at the Henderson hall grounds.

NEW YORK SUN
August 8, 1906

ARREST SALISBURY LYNCHERS.

SALISBURY, N.C., Aug. 7.—The bodies of Ness Gillespie, Jack Dillingham and John Gillespie, who were lynched a mile east of Salisbury last night, were today viewed by Coroner Borsett and taken down from the limb to which they had been hanged. The jail today is a wreck.

The two Misses Lyerly, the only ones of the family of seven who escaped death on the night of the murder, last night visited the scene of the lynching and viewed the bodies of the victims dangling in the moonshine.

Gov. Glenn has called out two more military companies to assist the Rowan Rifles in holding the lynchers fast as they are arrested. John Hall was arrested today and the Sheriff has the names of many others who will be arrested. It is feared there will be trouble, the sentiment against the prosecution of the lynchers being strong.

RICHMOND (VA) TIMES-DISPATCH
August 15, 1906

SOUVENIR CARDS OF LYNCHED NEGROES.

(Special to The Times-Dispatch.)
SALISBURY, N.C., August 14.—A quantity of souvenir postal cards, bearing the photographs of the Gillespie and Dillingham negroes lynched here last week, have been mailed in the Salisbury post office, and Postmaster Ramsey is having the matter investigated as to whether or not the gruesome pictures are mailable. All the matter is being held pending an investigation by the Washington authorities.

The personal property of the late Isaac Lyerly, whose family was murdered near Barbers Junction, July 13th, was sold at public auction today. A large crowd attended the sale, and much of the property sold at good prices. The dwelling has been unoccupied since the night of the tragedy.

BRECKENRIDGE NEWS (CLOVERPORT, KY)
August 22, 1906

NEGRO LYNCHED WHILE THE GOVERNOR PLEADED TO SAVE HIM.

COLUMBIA, S.C., Aug. 17.—Within the shadow of the home of his victim, Miss Jennie Brooks, after having been identified by her and after Governor Haywood addressed the mob in vain, Bob

Davis, the negro who murderously attacked Miss Brooks Aug. 12 with intent to commit assault, and who afterward outraged a negro girl 14-years-old, was lynched at Greenwood, Thursday night.

Governor Haywood reached the scene shortly after the negro was captured. A platform was erected in a fence corner on the premises of the victim's father, from which platform Governor Haywood addressed the mob in an effort to prevent the lynching. The governor beseeched the mob not to lynch Davis. At the conclusion of his speech, the governor was vociferously cheered. The mob then removed the prisoner from the view of the governor and within a short distance of the home of his victim; the negro was riddled with bullets.

THE (BOSTON) INDEPENDENT

August 23, 1906

RECENT LYNCHINGS IN THE SOUTH.

Robert Davis, a negro, was lynched in Greenwood, S. C. on the 16th, four days after the conviction at Salisbury, N. C., of George B. Hall, who was sent to prison for fifteen years for leading a mob that lynched three negroes at that place. Davis had committed an assault upon Miss Jennie Brooks, a young white woman, the daughter of a Greenwood merchant, and afterward had attacked a young negro girl. Those who captured him were preparing' to burn him at the stake when Governor Heyward, who had come hurriedly from the capital, addressed them from an improvised platform, urging that the law be permitted to take its course and promising that the man should be tried within two weeks before a Greenwood jury.

He was cheered by the lynchers, but at the same time, they expressed their determination to kill Davis. Their only concession was the substitution of shooting for burning. In answer to her own request, the mother of the injured negro girl was permitted to fire the first shot. The negroes of Greenwood County have published an address denouncing Davis and expressing approval of the lynchers' action.

It appears that the Salisbury militia had ball cartridges when on guard at the jail from which the three negroes were taken, on the

6th, and that the sheriff gave orders that they should not be used. It is reported that Governor Glenn will issue an order instructing military officers to act upon their own responsibility in such cases, when a sheriff refuses to direct that force be used for the protection of prisoners. Hundreds of souvenir postal cards, bearing photographs of the lynched negroes as they were hanging from the trees, were held at the Salisbury post office until the Department at Washington should decide whether they could be forwarded in the mails. The decision was that they were not mailable. By the North Carolina press, generally the lynching of the negroes at Salisbury is denounced and the prosecution and punishment of Hall are approved.

On the other hand, the *Atlanta News,* owned by Governor Terrell's chief of staff, says that "nothing short of the stake would have meted proper punishment to" the negroes lynched at Salisbury, commends the Greenwood lynchers, and offers $1,000 reward for the lynching of any negro who assaults a white woman in Atlanta. On the 20th, three days after this offer was made, a mob, intent upon earning the reward, was hunting in Atlanta for a negro accused of assaulting two young white girls, Ethel and Mabel Lawrence, daughters of a well known citizen.

EVENING NEWS (ADA, OK)

August 25, 1906

LYNCHING SOUVENIRS.

Souvenir postal cards bearing pictures of two negroes as they appeared swinging from the limb of a tree on the morning after they were lynched have been mailed to Salisbury, N.C., which place apparently take pride in the lynching. The postal cards have been held up pending a decision by the department authorities in Washington whether such things can properly be transmitted through the mails. There ought to be no doubt about the decision.— *Kansas City Journal.*

THE BEE (EARLINGTON, KY)

September 6, 1906

LYNCHING AND BUSINESS. CRIMES OF NEGROES ON LEVEL WITH MOB LAW, SAY WASHINGTON.

ATLANTA, Ga., Aug. 3.—Booker T. Washington, in his annual address before the Nation Negro Business League here, declared that lynching is the greatest enemy of business, and that crimes of negroes are on a level with mob law. He declared that the world does not respect a cringing, whining race. He declared it was the negroes' duty to stop crimes. He said in part:

"On the negroes part we have a duty. Our leaders should see to it that the criminal negro is gotten rid of whenever possible. One of the elements in our present situation that gives me the most concern is the large number of crimes that are being committed by members of our race. The negro is committing too much crime, north and south. The crime of lynching is everywhere and at all times should be condemned, and those who commit crimes of any nature should be condemned. Our Southland today has no greater enemy to business progress than lynchers and those who provoke lynching. We cannot be too frank or too strong in discussing the harm that the committing of crime is doing to our race. Let us stand up straight and speak out, and act in no uncertain terms in this direction. Let us do our part, and then let us call the whites to do their part."

TITUSVILLE (PA) HERALD
October 9, 1906

BELIEVED THAT CROWD LYNCHED NEGRO. AT ARGENTA—800 NEGROES SPENT NIGHT AT LITTLE ROCK.

KANSAS CITY, Mo., October 8.—A special to the Journal from Little Rock says:

Blackburn, the negro taken from the jail by a mob at Argenta, Ark., last night and lynched, is not believed to have been the man wanted. Fully 800 negroes deserted their homes in Argenta, and came to Little Rock to spend the night. The leaders stated that they were afraid to remain in Argenta for fear of another outbreak by the whites.

WASHINGTON POST
October 13, 1906

MOB SPIRIT IN CHILDREN.

The Spartanburg lynching bee presents another aspect of the motives that inspire mobs to bloody, law-defying deeds. In their efforts to get at a negro accused of a crime and already in jail, the Spartanburgers shot the sheriff.

They were willing to sacrifice a valuable, law-defending life in order to destroy a worthless one. However, in their battle with the authorities one of their own number was shot. He was a boy 14 years of age. And here comes the wonder of it—that he was not wounded accidentally or as an innocent bystander in the way of stray bullets, but as a leader in the riot. In fact, he is said to have been assisting in the act of battering down the doors of the jail.

It is to be hoped that there is some mistake in the report. But at least the incident points to the very marrow of the mob spirit, and reveals it in all its viciousness. It is impossible to conceive of an average 14-Year-old boy so filled with a sense of outraged justice, that he would willingly offer his life in the effort to discourage crime in his community. The only probable motive that could induce a boy of such tender age to lead a mob and endeavor to batter down the doors of the jail in order to get at his victim would be that of mere thirst for blood, *a desire* to satisfy it with human life.

This brutalizing of boys is one of the *very worst results of lynchings*. It breeds a carnival spirit of glee at the violent death of another, which is little short *of* fiendish. If there were no other reason why lynching should be regarded as one of the most terrible crimes which a community could commit, this one reason would be sufficient, that it brutalizes the young men and children who come in contact with it. The very ghouls of hell must shudder at the spectacle of children taking part in the efforts of a mob to burn a human being at the stake or hang him to a tree.

THE JIMPLECUTE (JEFFERSON, TX)

November 3, 1906

A MISSISSIPPI LYNCHING. NEGRO FOUND CUTTING HEAD OFF HIS VICTIM IS STRUNG UP.

NEW ORLEANS, La., Tom Crompton, a negro, was lynched near Centerville, Miss. It is alleged that he confessed to the murder of Ely Whitaker, a farmer. Whitaker was murdered Tuesday, and all Tuesday night a posse of men, suspecting foul play, searched for him. With this posse was the negro Crompton. Wednesday, he begged leave from the searchers to go home, but after he had gone the posse followed him, finding, it is alleged, that instead of going home he had gone to the spot where Whitaker's body lay, and cutting the head, arms, and legs with an ax, had dropped them into a sink near his cabin.

BOURBON NEWS (PARIS, KY)

November 9, 1906

ON FORBIDDEN GROUND.

Western Texas has had its first lynching. Negroes are barred from the town of Toyah, and from a surrounding radius of 100 miles. The negro, who was lynched, offended against this rule, agreed upon many years ago, and was strung up to the cross arm of a telegraph pole.

Slab Pitt was the offender. It might not have gone so hard with him had he left town when notified. Instead, he sent over into New Mexico and got a white woman with whom he had been living, to join him at Toyah. From the hour of her arrival, his fate was sealed.

On the appointed night, cowboys came in from all directions, each with a lariat on the pommel of his saddle. Pitt was brought from his home and hanged without ceremony. A purse was then made up for the white woman, and she was ordered to leave town on the first train. She went.

BALTIMORE SUN

December 23, 1906

VICTIM THANKS LYNCHERS IN LETTER TO ANNAPOLIS PAPER. DAUGHTER'S NAME SIGNED TO IT.

[Special Dispatch to the *Baltimore Sun.*]

Annapolis, Md., Dec. 22.—In a statement given out today Miss Lillian M. Reid, of Iglehart's Station, daughter of Mrs. John M. Reid, the victim of the negro Davis, who was lynched early yesterday morning, says that her mother is still confined to bed, extremely ill, as the result of the assault on Friday, December 14, and that here recovery, it is feared, is doubtful. The following communication to the Evening Capital today is signed with Miss Reid's name:

"We heard that the people of and near Annapolis, at an early hour this morning (the communication is drafted yesterday) brought out the negro and hanged him and then filled him full of shot.

"Would you please say to the kind people of Annapolis that we all thank them very much for what they have done? For it was not only for my mother's good, but for that of every woman, and my mother bids me to say that is she were only able she would like to shake each one by the hand, but as she is so very weak I can only tell you what she say. It was a dreadful, bold thing to do in broad daylight, and my mother is still in a very weak condition. We hope and pray for her recovery, but it is feared to be doubtful."

Much regret has been expressed that the lynching took place within a quarter of a mile of the home of Governor Warfield, who a few months ago took such great precaution to have a negro, guilty of practically the same crime committed in Somerset County, hanged on Smith's Island, in Chesapeake Bay, to avoid a possible lynching.

It is a source of much regret at St. John's College that the statement has been made that a number of students of that institution participated in the lawless act, and it is stated on high authority that such was not the case. The lynching party forming, as it did, almost in the midst of the students' dormitory, naturally attracted some of them, who through mere curiosity, followed the crowd and witnessed the proceedings. That the college grounds were chosen as the place for rendezvous has been pointed out to implicate the students, the support of this being that the grounds are not a desirable place for the meeting for such a purpose,. but it will be remembered that in 1898, when the mob of more than 100 men from North Tavern came to town and lynched the negro Wright Smith it formed there and laid the plans for attack upon the jail. The rear campus is a dark place and seldom does a pedestrian pass over it late at night, so that it is well adapted for the assembling of a mob.

A local photographer, who succeeded yesterday in getting pictures of the dead negro's body as it lay on the embankment of College Creek, where the lynchers deserted it, has printed copies on postal cards. Today they found ready sale, at two for 25 cents, as souvenirs.

EVENING CAPITAL

December 24, 1906

WHAT OTHERS THINK. COMMENTS OF THE PRESS ON THE RECENT LYNCHING EPISODE.

As stated in the Capital's editorial the day of the lynching of Henry Davis, the town and this State are now being made the target for criticism shot at it by the press throughout the country.

The *New York Sun* of December 22 says editorially:

"The negro who was lynched in Annapolis yesterday morning was led by the mob through the streets of the quarter inhabited by his race, "as an object lesson to the population there." The sight must have had a tremendous effect on men of his color. They learned from it that the State of Maryland was incapable of guarding its public institutions, which are at the mercy of any "two or three score of men" who meet at midnight to invade a community, overpower the officers of the law and do what they please with the persons committed to the guardianship of the State. One result of this "object lesson" will be to bring the legal processes of the State into contempt with the very class it is most desirable to impress with their strength and power."

The *American Magazine* says:

"No one can look at one of the photographs of a lynching without a sense of abysmal horror. It is not the horror alone or chiefly of the thing itself, the ugly, inanimate center of the tragedy. It is the faces of the spectators that shock our very souls. They are always laughing faces. Good nature, even jollity, seems to be the note of these gatherings. Always we see the faces of little boys grinning cheerfully toward the camera. There are women sometimes in the crowd, and sometimes little girls. there is no sign in these pictures of horror of death, even of girls. There is no sign in these pictures of horror of death, even of grim satisfaction over a difficult and obnoxious task performed by necessity. The man who called it a "lynching bee" appreciated the true feelings of the lynchers. Leave out the grim wreck in the center, and the picture might be taken for an ordinary cheerful gathering at a county fair. Leave it in, and oh, my brothers! It is not the dead, but the living that terrifies."

BRECKENRIDGE (CLOVERPORT, KY) NEWS
January 16, 1907

A WHITE WIFE-MURDERER LYNCHED.

CHARLES CITY, Iowa, Jan. 10.—James Cullen, who murdered his wife and 15-year-old stepson, was taken from the Floyd County jail here by a mob and hanged to the Cedar River Bridge, in the heart of the city. The mob broke into the jail, and quickly overpowered the feeble resistance that Sheriff Schermerhorn was able to offer.

The mob was composed of many of the leading citizens of the town, and even the leaders made no attempt to disguise themselves. Cullen fought like a tiger, but was overpowered. He declared that his wife and son had attacked him, and that he had killed them in self-defense. Four or five ministers, and a large number of women were in the crowd.

THE FALLS CITY (NEBRASKA) TRIBUNE
January 25, 1907

TO HELL WITH THE LAW!

When Senator Tillman was reminded that lynching negroes was against the law he replied, "to hell with such law." Senator Tillman is one of the lawmakers of this great and glorious country of freedom and equal rights.

HOPKINSVILLE KENTUCKIAN
March 7, 1907

NEGROES ARE SERVED IN RESTAURANT OF HOUSE.

Southerners are indignant because the other day for the first time in the memory of members of congress negroes have been served at the House of Representatives restaurant.

While several southern men were dining in the portion reserved for members and their guests, a negro accompanied by a white woman entered. The couple took seats at an adjoining table, and ordered food as coolly as though they had no idea of the precedent they were smashing.

The negro waiters served them with alacrity. Adamson, of Georgia; Randell of Louisiana; Taylor of Alabama, and a few other southerners were dining in the same room. Representative Weeks, of Massachusetts, and Gardner of Michigan, at an adjoining table, waited to see what the southern members would do. They did nothing. They continued to eat without starting a lynching bee.

After they had returned to the Democratic cloakroom, they decided to "cut out" dining in the house restaurant hereafter. "We are not in the habit of dining with negroes," said one of them, "and we don't propose to do it now even if it is permitted at the capitol."

And only Saturday Senator Tillman, of South Carolina, gloated over the fact that there were places in Washington where negroes "could not drink with white men, and you senators know it is true."

"It is a good thing Senator Tillman was not eating in there when the colored man sat down," commented one of the negro waiters after the restaurant episode had occurred, "because there sure would have been something doing."

"NEGROES ARE SERVED IN RESTAURANT OF HOUSE."
Hopkinsville Kentuckian, March 07, 1907, pg. 7.

CEDAR RAPIDS EVENING GAZETTE

June 19, 1907

WOMEN LED MOB OF LYNCHERS FINED AND SENT TO JAIL FOR TRYING TO HANG A MAN.

ASSUMPTION, Ill., June 19.—Fifteen warrants have been issued for the arrest of persons who attempted to lynch Alfred Bouland. Victor Ritchie, Josephine Ritchie, and Jane Sorrows, alleged leaders of the mob, were sentenced to jail and heavily fined.

Bouland, who married a woman here six months ago, had a wife in the old country. The latter arrived two weeks ago and Bouland has been in jail, charged with bigamy, but was released on bond. Upon returning to Assumption, he was set upon by a mob with knives, revolvers, and clubs. One woman had a rope around the victim's neck when officers arrive and beat off the mob.

LA CROSSE (WISCONSIN) TRIBUNE

June 25, 1907

REFUSE TO BE FREE. WOULD-BE WOMEN LYNCHERS FIGHT FOR PRINCIPLE

ASSUMPTION, Illinois, June 25.—Six women of Assumption, five of them mothers of families, and one a girl of 17, are in jail at Taylorsville, sixteen miles from their homes, and they say they will stay there until the morality of their town is vindicated. With a word, they could gain freedom, but they are fighting for a principle.

The have sent this message to their husbands and relatives in Assumption: "Do not come to us. Do not try to get bond for us until you have driven that bad man away." The "bad man" is Alfred Bourland, whom the six women, led by his "wife number one," Eugenie, attempted to lynch at Assumption, because they believed he was a bigamist. They must remain in jail a year if the refuse to accept bond.

TIMES-DISPATCH (RICHMOND, VA)

July 30, 1907

DIG UP AND BURN A LYNCHED NEGRO.

CRISFIELD, MD., July 29.—With their passion impossible to satisfy by the kicking and beating to death of the negro Reed, who on Saturday evening, without provocation, shot and killed Policeman Daugherty, who had Reed's associate, William Hilldred, under arrest, a mob at an early hour today dug up Reed's mutilated remains from the rude grave in a swamp near town, into which they had been thrown, riddled the remains with bullets, and then, lighting a bonfire, tossed them into the flames and stood around watching until they were reduced to ashes.

Lemuel Showers, the keeper of a billiard-room frequented by negroes, who loaned Reed the revolver with which he shot Daugherty, was captured today and lodged in the county jail at Princess Anne. Every train arriving at Crisfield was searched, in the hope that Showers would be found on board.

Had he been found, he would almost certainly have been lynched, because there has been much trouble with lawless negroes, and the feeling against such is very high. Hilldred, who arrest precipitated the trouble, has not yet been captured. When he is, the authorities will undoubtedly keep him away from this city, or else he would sure meet a fate similar to Reed's.

NEGROES COMMEND LYNCHING.

There has been no adverse criticism of the treatment given to Reed. Those who put an end to his life stung his body up to a telegraph pole, and, after the inquest interred him in the swamp, yesterday did their work without attempt at concealment. It was no party of masked men, but a band of citizens whose patience had been tried too far by the lawless negroes of this locality. Even among the colored race the work of the lynchers met approval.

Today the Town Council was waited upon by a delegation representing the best colored element of the vicinity, and including all the local colored ministers and a colored physician. They asked to be allowed to cooperate with the white citizens in restoring order and proper feeling between blacks and whites.

They asked that the Council close all places of business and amusement where the unruly element among the blacks might congregate and foment trouble. They offered to furnish information upon which certain places in the negro section might be closed. They presented resolutions expressing regret for the murder of Daugherty and commending him; condemned Reed and his kind, and said that they would have been willing to join in the hunt for him, and in lynching him when he was captured.

PALESTINE (TEXAS) DAILY HERALD
July 19, 1907

OSAGE INDIANS ASSISTED IN LYNCHING NEGRO WHO KILLED BRAKEMAN FEW NIGHTS AGO.

[Special to the Herald.]
GUTHRIE, Okla., July 17.—It has been developed that a number of Osage Indians participated in the lynching of Frank Bailey, the negro. Tuesday night, Bailey killed a brakeman who was trying to make him get off a train.

SAN FRANCISCO (CA) CALL
July 19, 1907

FEDERAL GOVERNMENT IS TO PROSECUTE LYNCHERS.

GUTHRIE, Oklahoma, July 18.—For the first time in the history of Oklahoma the government will prosecute lynchers. United States Marshal John Abernathy and two assistant United States attorneys are in Osage, Oklahoma, tonight securing evidence against the members of the mob, which on Tuesday night hanged a negro, Frank Bailey, for assaulting Brakeman Frank Kelley. Charges of murder will be preferred against the men and boys in the mob. Osage is in an Indian reservation, and the territorial authorities have no jurisdiction.

PALESTINE (TEXAS) DAILY HERALD
July 20, 1907

NUMBER OF LYNCHERS ARRESTED.

GUTHRIE, Oklahoma, July 20.—Federal officers arrested six members of the mob, which is alleged to have lynched Frank Bailey, a negro, Tuesday night, after he had killed a brakeman for refusing to let him ride on a freight train. A charge of murder has been filled against each of them.

PALESTINE (TEXAS) DAILY HERALD
July 25, 1907

KATY OFFICIALS WILL DEFEND EMPLOYEES, IMPRISONED ON CHARGE OF LYNCHING NEGRO.

[Special to the *Herald*.]

Guthrie, Oklahoma, July 25.—Prominent officials of the Missouri, Kansas and Texas Railroad today assured three employees who are in the Federal prison here on the charge of participating in a mob which lynched a negro who shot one of the company's brakemen, that the Railroad has $90,000 with which to defend the prisoners.

SHENANDOAH HERALD (WOODSTOCK, VA)
August 2, 1907

NEGRO LYNCHED IN MARYLAND.

Night Policeman John H. Daugherty, of Crisfield, Md., was shot and instantly killed Saturday night by Jas. reed, a half negro and half Indian, while conveying the negro prisoner to the lock up.

Reed escaped, but was captured in Tangier Sound Sunday. He was taken to Crisfield, and as soon as he was put ashore, he was attacked by an infuriated mob, which kicked him to death. His body was suspended from a telephone pole, where it remained for some time in full gaze of all passersby. The coroner's jury met after the body was cut down. The verdict implicated no one.

VIRGINIA CITIZEN (IRVINGTON, VA)

August 2, 1907

DUG UP LYNCHED NEGRO.

With their passions unsatisfied by the kicking and beating to death of a negro, Reed, at Crisfield, Md., who on Saturday evening, without provocation, shot and killed Policeman Daugherty, who had Reed's associate under arrest. A mob dug up Reed's mutilated remains from the rude grave in a swamp near town, into which, they had thrown it, riddled it with bullets, and then, lighting a bonfire tossed the corpse into the flames, and stood about watching until they were reduced to ashes.

Lemuel Showers, the keeper of a billiard-room frequented by negroes, who loaned Reed the revolver with which he shot Daugherty, was captured today at Princess Anne. Every train arriving at Crisfield was searched, in the hope that Showers would be found on board. Had he been, he would almost certainly have been lynched. For there has been much trouble with lawless negroes, and the feeling against such is very high. Hilldred, whose arrest precipitated the trouble, has not yet been captured. When he is, the authorities will undoubtedly keep him away; else, he would surely meet a fate similar to Reed's.

There has been no adverse criticism of the treatment given Reed. Those who put an end to his life, stung his body up to a telegraph pole, and after the inquest interred him in the swamp. They did their work without attempt at concealment. It was no party of masked men, but a band of citizens whose patience had been tried too far by the lawless negroes of that locality. Even among the colored race, the work of the lynchers met approval.

LOS ANGELES (CALIFORNIA) HERALD
September 3, 1907

OKLAHOMA LYNCHERS NOT GRANTED BAIL.

GUTHRIE—Judge John H. Buford in chambers refused to permit the released on bond of Red Williams, C.A. Green, and Michael White, held on charges of murder in connection with the lynching of Frank Bailey. In the case of Everett Stover, on the charge of killing Tom Stewart in the Osage Nation, his release on $5000 bond was ordered.

LOS ANGELES HERALD
December 14, 1907

WHITE MEN GUARD NEGROES.

[By Associated Press.]

CARROLLTON, Ala., Dec. 13.—Scores of white citizens of Carrollton stood guard all of last night over the church and schoolhouse for negroes in this town and at the county jail. The action was due to reports that a mob of white men was coming to Carrollton, to take the negro who incited the trouble at Fords from jail and lynch him.

PADUCAH (KENTUCKY) EVENING SUN
December 19, 1907

NO LYNCHING IN KENTUCKY AT ALL. RECORD OF THE U.S. FOR YEAR IS ONLY 42.

CHICAGO, Ill., Dec. 19.—The lynching record for 1907 will show a decided improvement over that of 1906. The total for the current year to date is 42—3 negro women, 4 white men, and 35 negro men. The record includes only cases of unmistakable lynching, leaving out those in which the victims were killed by pursuing posses while resisting capture. The record last year was 72, being 30 more than that of 1907.

Crimes charged against those lynched range from robbery to assault and murder. It is worthy of notice that none of the victims were lynched for such petty or trivial crimes as in some previous years. A large majority of the victims were guilty of criminal assault or attempted criminal assault.

The lynchings were most numerous in Alabama, Georgia, Mississippi, and Louisiana. Father north there was two lynchings in Maryland, and one each in Missouri, Iowa, and Nebraska.

Altogether, there were lynchings in 12 states. The larger number occurred in the hot summer months.

OCALA (FLORIDA) EVENING STAR
December 26, 1907

OKLAHOMA'S FIRST LYNCHING. SINCE IT BECAME A STATE OCCURRED CHRISTMAS EVE.

MUSKOGEE, Okla., Dec. 26.—Riddled with bullets, the body of James Garden, a negro, is dangling from a telegraph pole in Henrietta, Okla., a coal mining town thirty mile west of here, as the result of the first lynching in the new state. Garden shot and killed Albert Bates, a white man, because Bates, who is a well-known clergyman, refused to rent a rig to the negro. Garden said Bates was discriminating against him because of his color, and going across the street for a pistol, Garden returned and killed Bates. Garden was lodged in jail and a mob of 100 men battered down the doors of the jail, secured the negro, and hung him to a nearby pole. They then riddled the body with bullets.

NEW YORK EVENING WORLD
January 3, 1908

1908'S FIRST LYNCHING.

BROOKHAVEN, Miss., Jan. 3.—Probably the first lynching of 1908 took place here yesterday when a mob in broad daylight took a negro away from police officers and shot him. The negro was accused of killing a policeman at Oak Vale.

The men got the negro away from the police by using a lariat, which was thrown over his neck as the officers were taking him to jail. The lassoing took place near the central part of town.

NEW BRUNSWICK TIMES
January 21, 1908

LIVES AFTER BEING HANGED. LYNCHED BY MOB, NEGRO REVIVES AFTER BEING STRUNG UP ALL NIGHT.

DOTHAN, Ala., Jan. 21.—Cleveland Franklin, a negro, has undergone the terrible experience of being lynched and lives to tell how he felt when being hanged by a mob.

Franklin, who shot and dangerously wounded A.C. Faulk, a leading business man of this place, was taken from the sheriff by 200 masked men, hanged to a tree in the public square and at least 200 shots fired at his dangling body.

The body remained suspended all night, and until late in the morning, when it was cut down by the coroner. In examining the body the coroner found signs of life, and hc summoned physicians, who soon had the negro talking. It was found that out of the hundreds of bullets fired only six had taken effect, and they had not inflicted even dangerous wounds. His clothing, however, had been almost stripped from him by the bullets. The noose around the negro's neck had not been properly adjusted and failed to strangle him.

PADUCAH (KENTUCKY) EVENING SUN
February 10, 1908

MILITIA OVERPOWERED BY ENRAGED CITIZENS.

MEMPHIS, Tenn., Feb. 10.—Ell Pigot, a negro, was lynched at Brookhaven Miss., today. He confessed to assaulting Nellie Williams, a white girl, eighteen years old. He was taken to Brookhaven for trial, and the militia accompanied him. Tom Williams, the father, wanted to see the negro, and a soldier knocked him down. The enraged crowd swept the militia aside, dragged the negro from the car, and hanged him to a telephone pole.

POVERTY BAY HERALD (GISBORNE, NEW ZEALAND)

March 14, 1908

AMERICAN NEWS. NEGROES LYNCH A NEGRO.

January 16.—A mob of negroes at Pine Bluff, a small hamlet in Johnston County, lynched an unknown negro. The negro, purporting to be an advance agent of a "big show," induced the negro residents into attendance on what turned out to be a one-man performance by the "agent" himself. Their heads covered with guano sacks, the mob entered the negro's boarding house early Thursday morning, and took him to the woods. His body was found at daylight on the Southern Railroad tracks.

RENO EVENING GAZETTE

March 21, 1908

GRUESOME LYNCHING PICTURES.

HANGING in the window of Rosenthal & Armanko's store of Virginia Street is a picture of "Ortiz," the Mexican, who was lynched in this city in 1891 for shooting Richard Hahn, at the time the constable of Reno. The picture shows Ortiz standing erect in a pine coffin with the rope around his neck. this was the first and only lynching party ever held in the city of Reno.

NEW YORK TIMES

July 29, 1908

NEGRO BURNED AT STAKE. FIRE BUILT IN PUBLIC SQUARE AT GREENVILLE, TEXAS.

DALLAS, Texas, July 29.—"Tad" Smith, a negro boy, 18 years old, charged with criminal assault on Miss Viola Delancey at Clinton, Hunt County, yesterday afternoon, was captured by officers early today.

He was taken before the young woman and identified, and the officers hurried with him toward the Greenville Jail. A mob of citizens overpowered them, took the prisoner, and prepared to hang him. After a discussion, the mob agreed to burn him at the stake. Fagots were piled up in the public squared at Greenville, and the negro was placed thereon. Kerosene oil was poured on, and a match applied. Smith slowly burned to death while 1,000 persons looked on.

PALESTINE (TEXAS) DAILY HERALD
August 1, 1908

FOUR NEGROES HANGED BY THE NECK.

[Special to the *Herald*.]

RUSSELLVILLE, Ky., Aug. 1.—A mob of several hundred men took four negroes from the county jail at an early hour this morning, and lynched them. The victims were Virgil Jones, Tom Jones, Joe Riley, and Robert Jones. The murder of Jas Cunningham, a white farmer, by Rufus Browder, a negro, because he was discharged, was the direct cause of the lynching.

Browder is now in Louisville Jail awaiting trial for the murder of Cunningham. The negroes lynched were members of the lodge, which adopted resolutions indorsing the murder of Cunningham by the negro. The mob, after swinging the negroes, pinned warnings of the bodies, warning other negroes to be good.

PENSACOLA (FL) JOURNAL
August 1, 1908

PICTURES OF LYNCHED NEGRO. VIOLATION OF LAW TO SEND THEM TROUGH MAILS AS POST CARDS.

"It is a violation of the United States laws to send such photographs through the mails as post cards," said a United States official yesterday in referring to the pictures of the negro Shaw, whose photograph had been taken after the lynching showing numerous bullet holes in the body.

The official in question stated that under the recent act of congress anything of this nature is not permitted to be sent out as postal cards, and that citizens of Pensacola should bear this in mind, as it is likely that a number will wish to forward them to friends in adjoining cities. Photographers, who took the photograph of the negro as he lay in the undertaker's casket, have had a rush of orders for pictures, many desiring them as souvenirs of the lynching.

KKK cross-burning rally in the above picture, date unknown. The Ku Klux Klan caused many African Americans to live in fear during the late 1890s-1960s. The Klan often utilized intimidation tactics through the use of violence, cross burnings ect.

SAN FRANCISCO CALL
October 5, 1908

MOB LYNCHES NEGRO FAMILY.

HICKMAN, KY., Oct. 4.—Dave Walker, a negro, his 5 year old daughter, and his baby child, were killed outright. The mother, who was holding the baby in her arms, was fatally shot and three other children will probably die, as a result of a mob's visit to the Walker home near her, late last night.

In addition, the oldest son is missing and is supposed to have been burned by the mob. Walker had cursed at a white woman, and threatened a white man with a pistol. When the mob of 50 men ordered him to come from his house, he replied with a shot. The torch was then applied to the house, and as the occupants came out they were shot down.

COMMERCE (TEXAS) JOURNAL
September 25, 1908

NEGROES LYNCH NEGRO.

YAZOO CITY, Miss., Sept. 20.—Negroes today shot and killed Charles Jones, a member of their own race, who yesterday killed a white man and two negroes at Eden Station, Miss. The negroes found Jones at his residence, and shot him as he was trying to escape. They also have made threats of lynching the person who sold Jones the cocaine, which is believed to have caused his murderous outbreak. Thus far, the identity of the cocaine seller has not been learned.

PALESTINE (TX) DAILY HERALD
October 7, 1908

Ben Price, a negro, was hung by a mob at Glen Flora, Texas for criminal assault on his daughter.

FARMVILLE HERALD (FARMVILLE, VA)
December 4, 1908

A LEGALIZED TRIPLE LYNCHING.

The town of Tiptonville, Tenn., bordering on Realfoot Lake, which recently has been the scene of many stirring incidents, witnessed the "legalized " lynching of 3 negroes who were arrested for murdering Special Deputy sheriff Richard Burruss on Sunday, and also wounding John Hall, a deputy sheriff. The execution of the negroes was given a semblance of legality by a hurried "trial," arranged with the understanding that the men would be condemned to death as soon as the "trial" was over.

The negroes lynched were Marshall Stineback, Edward Stineback, and James Stineback. These three brothers created a disturbance at a religious meeting near Tiptonville on Saturday night. When Officers Burruss and Hall attempted to arrest them the negroes shot the officers.

PALESTINE (TEXAS) DAILY HERALD
January 12, 1909

A BAD NEGRO LYNCHED.

[Special to the *Herald*]

SHREVEPORT, LA., JAN.—12.—Jud Gilbert, known as a bad negro, was lynched at Marthasville last night. He was arrested as a counterfeiter. A mob stormed the jail and lynched him. Gilbert lived in a cabin, which was fitted up as an arsenal, and had been a terror to the community for years.

WINCHESTER (KY) NEWS,
January 15, 1909

LYNCHINGS IN 1908.

The number of lynchings in 1907 was the smallest in twenty years, being but sixty-three. It is not encouraging that the number in 1908 was 100, the largest number since 1903. As the lynching evil is a problem of national interest, the following table is appended showing the annual number for the last twenty-four years:

1885	184	1897	166
1886	138	1898	127
1887	122	1899	107
1888	142	1900	115
1889	176	1901	135
1890	127	1902	96
1891	192	1903	104
1892	235	1904	87
1893	200	1905	66
1894	190	1906	69
1895	171	1907	63
1896	131	1908	100

PALESTINE (TEXAS) DAILY HERALD
January 12, 1909

BAD NEGRO LYNCHED.

SHREVEPORT, La., Jan. 12.—Jud Gilbert, known as a bad negro, was lynched at Mathaville last night. He was arrested as a counterfeiter. A mob stormed the jail and lynched him. Gilbert lived in a cabin, which was fitted up as an arsenal, and had been a terror to the community for years.

PADUCAH (KY) EVENING SUN
March 19, 1909

WHITE MAN LYNCHED.

ELKINS, W.Va., March 19.—Joe Brown, who shot and probably fatally injured Scott White, at Whitmer, was taken from the jail here this morning and lynched by 50 men. Brown was a white man.

Brown had been a fugitive from justice four years. He returned to Whitmer yesterday, and got into a fight with White, the chief of police. He drew a revolver and fired and escaped, but was later captured by a posse.

PALESTINE (TEXAS) DAILY HERALD
April 17, 1909

ESCAPED A LYNCHING. MOB HAD APPLIED TAR & FEATHERS TO NORTH DAKOTA MAN.

(Herald Special.)

Linton, N.D., April 17.—Tar and feather had been applied and a rope provided for hanging J. Bierman of Strasburg, N.D., today, when the sheriff arrived and saved him. Bierman is alleged to have attacked the 9-year-old daughter of Andrew Boschker. He was taken to jail with the tar and feathers still on him.

ALEXANDRIA (D.C.) GAZETTE
April 30, 1909

THREE MORE NEGROES LYNCHED.

DALLAS, Tex., April 30.—Three negroes were taken from the jail at Marshall, Texas, early today and hanged by a mob. They were accused of having killed Deputy Sheriff Huffman and wounding Deputy Sheriff Cargill, Monday. They were captured Tuesday after a long chase just as they were leaving the state. The men were taken to the jail at Marshall, where they were guarded by militia until it was thought the feeling against them had abated. The mob was formed after the militia had been sent away.

ALEXANDRIA (D.C.) GAZETTE
June 7, 1909

CHURCHGOERS VIEW LYNCHED NEGRO.

After having been tried, convicted, and sentenced to death for the murder of Sheriff Langdon, of Tallahassee, Florida, Mack Morris, a negro, was taken from the jail by a mob at two o'clock yesterday morning and hanged to a tree in front of the state capitol. As the negro was swinging the lynchers fired a volley into his body, and then rode away. There were about 100 men in the mob. The body was not cut down until early noon and was gazed at by hundreds on their way to the various churches. Governor Golchrist heard the volley fired by the lynchers, but he has made no statement.

THE CITIZEN (BEREA, KY)
May 13, 1909

NEGRO WAS HUNTED DOWN. PRISONER RIDDLED WITH BULLETS.

JACKSONVILLE, Fla., May 10.—In the presence of Mrs. Andrew Deas, whom he had assaulted, an unknown negro was lynched in the suburbs of Jacksonville early Sunday morning. The assault on Mrs. Deas was committed about dark Saturday evening. Mrs. Deas was on the grounds of her home when the negro sprang from behind shrubbery and seized her. she fought desperately, but the negro dragged her into the shrubbery. After the negro left, Mrs. Deas managed to reach the house and gave the alarm.

Her son organized a posse, and the negro was chased with dogs all Saturday night. He was captured about 4 o'clock some miles from the Deas home, and was hurried before Mrs. Deas for identification. "He is the negro," cried Mrs. Deas. As soon as Mrs. Deas announced that the right man had been captured, the posse began to pour volleys into the prisoner riddling his body.

Not satisfied with this, knives were used, and the negro's head almost severed from his body. The Sheriff was notified that there might be a lynching, and he hurried from Jacksonville to Deas' home, but when he reached there the mob had done its work, leaving the mutilated body of the negro in front of the Deas home.

SAN FRANCISCO (CALIFORNIA) CALL
August 16, 1909

NEGRO IS LYNCHED FOR SUING SLAYER OF COW.

MONROE, La., Aug. 15.—John Stoner, a negroe, sued a white man who killed his cow and was lynched because of his daring. The residents of Doss, near here, became angered because of the negro's action. The mob threatened him Thursday night, and the hanging followed.

SAN FRANCISCO (CALIFORNIA) CALL
August 16, 1909

SHERIFF PREVENTS LYNCHING.

AMERICUS, Ga., Aug. 15.—By a ruse, Sheriff Feagan outwitted a posse at DeSoto today, and in an automobile brought here Dean Adams, a negro, who confessed to attacking a white woman. Nothing but the sheriff's speedy car prevented a lynching.

ALEXANDRIA GAZETTE (ALEXANDRIA, D.C.)

September 3, 1909

TWO NEGROES LYNCHED.

MALCOLM, Ala., Sept. 3.—John and Lewis Balm, negroes, were lynched late last night near Jackson, Ala., for the murder of Sheriff J.L. Wainwright, according to a long distance telephone message received here today. The victim made a full confession.

CEDAR RAPID (IOWA) EVENING GAZETTE

November 12, 1909

HORRIFYING DETAILS OF CAIRO LYNCHING. HEAD OF NEGRO SEVERED; HEART CUT OUT & PIECES OF BLOOD-SOAKED ROPE USED AS SOUVENIRS.

CAIRO, Ill., Nov. 12.—The arrival of five companies of militia this morning apparently cowed the mob spirit, and no attempt has been made to storm the jail where is confined Arthur Alexander, the negro implicated by James in the killing of Miss Pelley. The jail is surrounded by soldiers while the adjoining streets are patrolled by detachments of troops.

Many citizens, while condemning the action of mobs, are satisfied with the night's work. Mayor Parson today said he did not anticipate further trouble.

GRUESOME SOUVENIRS.

Some incidents connected with the lynching of James are horrifying. Before the body was burned the negro's head was cut off and placed on a pole, one end of which was stuck in the ground. The heart was cut out of the body, cut up in pieces, and passed among the men as souvenirs. Pieces of the rope with which James was hanged and dragged, after being soaked in the negro's blood, were handed about as souvenirs.

HOPKINSVILLE KENTUCKIAN
November 16, 1909

LYNCHED NEGRO PADUCAH. THREE DIRECTLY CONNECTED WITH CAIRO MOB ARE WELL-KNOWN HERE

Frog James, the negro who was lynched for the murder of Annie Pelly, and Alexander, whom he implicated in his dying statement, are both Paducah negroes, and were run out of this city by the Paducah police. James was decidedly a police character, and gave the department here a great deal of trouble. He was a fishmonger while here, and peddled his catch on the streets. Alexander and he ran together here, just as they seem to have done in Cairo.—*News Democrat.*

ST. LUCIE COUNTY (FLORIDA) TRIBUNE
November 19, 1909

WORLD NEWS CONDENSED: HORRIFIC SOUVENIRS— THE CAIRO, ILLINOIS BURNING OF WILL JAMES.

To avenge the assault upon the murder of Miss Annie Pelley, of Cairo, Ill., a mob more frantic than any that has ever been formed in any State Thursday night lynched Will James, the negro accused of the crime. In addition, when the rope broke, 500 shots were poured into his body.

Women were present, and were the first to pull the rope. After the body had been horribly mutilated, the mob dragged it through the streets for a while, and then into an alley, where it was burned. Pieces of the rope were handed out as souvenirs, and the head of the negro was cut off, his heart taken out and cut into pieces for souvenirs. Gov. Deneen says that the affair is a disgrace to Illinois. The mob consisted of fully 5,000, and the women were seemingly the most conspicuous in the maddened crowd.

GIRL MURDERED BY BLACK FIEND

Annie Pelley, the girl slain by the negro, who was lynched in Cairo, Ill., with several women pulling on the rope. The mob, after hanging, shooting and burning the negro, also took a wife murderer from jail and strung him up. The Illinois militia prevented a third lynching.

Salt Lake Herald-Republican, (Salt Lake City, Utah), December 03, 1909, pg. 2. Caption reads: Annie Pelly, the girl slain by the negro, who was lynched in Cairo, Ill., with several women pulling on the rope. The mob, after hanging, shooting and burning the negro, also took a wife murderer from jail and strung him up too. The Illinois militia prevented a third lynching.

HOPKINSVILLE KENTUCKIAN
December 19, 1908

WHITE MAN. LYNCHED BY MOB FOR ATROCIOUS CRIME IN RUSSELL COUNTY.

DANVILLE, Ky., Dec. 17.—Elmer Hill, charged with the assault and murder of Mamie Womack, at Russell Springs, was taken from the jail at Monticello at 11 o'clock last night by a mob of 26 armed men, and placed behind one of the members of the mob on horseback. He was carried to a lonely spot on Greasy Creek, 6 miles away, and hanged to a sycamore tree. After sending several bullets through Hill's body the mob dispersed. The mob went 50 miles to get their man, and were forced to climb towering mountains, and cross Cumberland River.

The officers started to Lexington with Hill Monday morning, but, taking up the idea that a mob could not reach Monticello without being detected, returned the prisoner to the little jail at that point. The crime for which Hill was hanged was committed last Tuesday evening. The victim, a pretty twelve-year-old schoolgirl, was assaulted, her brains beaten out, her body carried into the woods and covered with leaves. Bloodhounds trailed Hill five days and covered a distance of 90 miles.

PALESTINE (TEXAS) DAILY HERALD
May 8, 1909

WRONG MAN LYNCHED.

TYLER, Texas, May 7.—It was announced here today that

District Judge Simpson had received an anonymous letter from Paris, in which the writer declares he attacked Miss Winnie Harmon, for which crime the negro Jim Hodge was lynched last Saturday.

NEW YORK TIMES
December 2, 1909

MOB BURNS NEGRO PREACHER. JOHN HARVARD HAD SHOT A WHITE AUTOIST WHO FRIGHTENED HIS MULES.

COCHRAN, Ga., Dec. 1—John Harvard, a negro preacher, who shot and fatally injured Will D. Booth, two miles from this place late this afternoon, was captured by a mob five miles from her tonight at 10 o'clock and burned at a stake, more than a carload of light wood, being heaped about the body.

Booth, who is a businessman of Hawkinsville, was en-route to Cochran in an automobile, and drove up behind Harvard, who was in a wagon. Harvard charged that Booth's machine frightened his mules. He drew a pistol after a few words, and fired upon Booth, three shots taking effect. Booth returned the fire, and it was learned after the negro was captured that he carried two bullets, but neither in vital spots. Booth was brought to this place soon after the shooting. Surgeons tonight gave out the statement that there was little hope for his recovery. He has a wife and several children.

Officers from Hawkinsville, in automobiles and carrying hounds went immediately to the scene of the shooting, but a party of citizens had been formed and had trailed the negro on horseback to his hiding place in a barn three miles away. He showed fight, but was suffering so severely for the effects of his injuries that he could offer little resistance. He freely admitted the shooting, and it is stated justified his action by the fact that Booth's automobile frightened his mules. He was given an opportunity to pray, after which he was securely bound with chains to an impoverished stake. The fuel was piled high above his head and the torch applied. The roaring of the flames prevented sound from being audible, if any escaped the man's lips.

THE BEE (EARLINGTON, KY)
January 27, 1910

BISHOP WARNS NEGROES.

NEW ORLEANS, La., Jan. 22.—"There are times when I can't blame mobs for lynching negroes," declared Bishop Hampton at the negro Methodist conference here.

"I appeal to every negro in the land to keep inviolate those lines of separation between the races in public and in private, so that mobs will have no excuse to wreak vengeance on my race.

"I appeal to every negro to keep from seeking any kind of intimacy by law of force, by agreement or intrigue, with the women of the other race.

"I do not seek admission into the parlor of any white man, nor do I invite him into my parlor in a social way. I want for my people only protection under law."

PALESTINE (TX) DAILY HERALD
March 18, 1910

TWO NEGROES LYNCHED.

MEMPHIS, Tenn., March 18.—Charles Richardson and Bob Austin, negroes, were taken from jail and hanged here this morning. The keys were taken from a deputy sheriff; the negroes removed from the jail by 50 men, and hanged to a tree in the jail yard. The mob dispersed without any excitement.

LOS ANGELES HERALD
March 20, 1910

CORONER SAYS LYNCHED NEGROES WERE

SUICIDES.

MARION, Ark., March 19.—According to the verdict of the coroner Bob Austen and Charley Richardson, the negroes lynched here yesterday charged with aiding and abetting a recent jail delivery "came to their death by suicide."

Preceding the lynching the town of Marion was reported to be threatened with a race riot. Later it developed that rioting was confined mainly to the stoning of negroes' houses by boys.

NEW YORK TIMES

July 23, 1910

NEGRO BURNED AT STAKE. PUT TO DEATH BY TEXAS MOB AFTER ATTACK ON WHITE WOMAN.

DALLAS, Texas, July 2.—Henry Gentry, a negro, who attempted to enter the room of a white woman at Belton, Texas, early this morning, and who later killed Constable James Mitchell who tried to arrest him, was burned at the stake tonight by a mob.

LOS ANGELES HERALD

August 25, 1910

HOLD WOMAN FOR PART IN ETHERINGTON LYNCHING.

ZANESVILLE, O., Aug. 24.—Mabel McManiway was arrested today and will be held for the Newark authorities in connection with the Etherington lynching on July 8th.

On the night of the lynching a thrill ran through the gathering around the gallows pole when a woman, standing on an automobile, shoved through the crowd into the very heart of the throng. Standing on the seat, she cried to the leaders:

"Pull him up a little higher so I can see."

PALESTINE (TX) DAILY HERALD
September 3, 1910

NEGRO STRUNG UP. 2,000 PEOPLE PARTICIPATE IN MISSISSIPPI LYNCHING.

Armory, Miss., Sept. 1.—Nick Thompson, a negro, accused of criminally assaulting a 17-year-old white girl at Jackson Crossing near here last Saturday, was taken to the scene of the crime this afternoon by a mob and lynched.

The lynching followed the identification of Thompson by Miss Jennie Jackson, his victim. As soon as the fact that the negro had been identified became known, the mob quickly formed, and hanged him to a telegraph pole. After accomplishing its purpose the mob dispersed.

NEW YORK TRIBUNE (NY, N.Y.)
September 3, 1910

LYNCH NEGRO MAN AND WOMAN.

GRACEVILLE, Fla., Sept. 2.—Dangling from a trestle just outside the town this morning were found the bodies of Edward Christian, a negro, charged with shooting Deputy Sheriff Allen Burns, and Hattie Bowman, a negress, who had been arrested on the charge of being implicated in the crime of murdering the sheriff.

THE DOTHAN (ALABAMA) EAGLE
October 4, 1910

NEGROES LYNCH ONE OF OWN RACE. ATTACKED A NEGRO WOMAN & HER FRIENDS FIND & KILL HIM.

TALLADEGA, AL., Oct. 3—Probably the first case of lynching by a mob of negroes alone without the aid and consul of white men, occurred near McFall Sunday, October 2, in this county. Thursday, a strange negro at a farm near Lincoln, fourteen miles from Talladega, assaulted a negro woman under circumstances of unusual atrocity.

The alarm was soon given, but the assailant escaped, going in an easterly direction on the road leading to McFall. The Lincoln negroes, consisting of friends and relatives of the woman assaulted made some efforts to procure a warrant, but for some reason they did not succeed in getting legal papers for the apprehension of the fleeing negro.

By a system of "grapevine telegraphy" peculiar to the negroes, tabs was kept on the trail of the assailant, and he was thought to be located Sunday near McFall, a station on the Georgia Pacific Division of the Southern road. Sunday, when the eastbound train on the Southern Railroad rolled into Lincoln, it was boarded by a number of negroes who had purchased tickets to McFall, and who were the relatives and neighbors of the outraged woman. They were not noisy or demonstrative, nor were any unusual number of weapons in evidence.

Arriving at McFall, they separated into groups, and began a quiet still hunt for the man. In a short time, they located a negro who answered the description previously obtained, and without any waste of time, they filled his body full of bullets and left him dead.

Will Thweatt, a merchant of McFall called up the Talladega authorities Monday, and notified them that there was a dead man, unburied near that place. Corner R. Heine procured an automobile and went there at 9:30 o'clock Monday morning.

It has been but a short time since the entire community around Lincoln was stirred over an assault upon a white woman by a negro. Several parties were arrested, and released upon preliminary trial, and it is not thought the right man has yet been apprehended. This circumstance gave rise to much talk of lynching among the people living near Lincoln, some of which was evidently heard by the negroes, which doubtless gave them the cue to take the law into their own hands in this instance.

The name of the man killed or the woman assaulted has not

been learned, but it is generally stated on the streets that the negro assailant was not a person belonging to that neighborhood. In the annals of the county, this is the first instance of where negroes have visited summary vengeance upon one of their own race for a crime against negro women, or any other crime.

MAHONING DISPATCH (CANFIELD, OH)
October 7, 1910

CROWD TAKES NEGRO FROM PRISON WARDEN & BURN NEGRO AT THE STAKE.

MONTGOMERY, Ala., Oct. 5.—Six hours after he had assaulted Mrs. Hiram Stuckey, a prominent young woman of Covington County, Bush Withers, a negro "trusty" at the Henderson convict camp, was taken from the warden while en-route to a prison at Andalusia, tied to a stake by a mob of 400 men and burned. The lynching was conducted quietly. The mob formed from adjoining towns and afterwards dispersed to their home, leaving no traces of their fury, except the ashes of the negro.

PADUCAH (KENTUCKY) EVENING SUN
November 10, 1910

MEXICANS LYNCH YOUNG AMERICAN.

SAN ANTONIO, Texas, Nov. 10.—Reports received here this morning from Mexico City, say that two Americans were killed in mob outbreaks late last night. Mobs, conducting the anti-Americans revolt, seized a young American on the outskirts of the city and lynched him to a tree, cutting down the body before the police arrived. An American child is reported killed when mobs stone a streetcar carrying Americans. Several Mexicans were killed by police suppressing the riots.

MUSCATINE (IOWA) JOURNAL
November 11, 1910

AMERICAN AND MEXICAN MOBS.

Chicago Tribune: The American government will call the attention of Mexico to the more violent and reprehensible features of the anti-American demonstrations in the city of Mexico. The Mexican government will express regret and promise to make every effort to punish guilty parties. The state department will demand satisfaction for injuries to unoffending American citizens, but it is painfully aware of the immediate cause of recent anti-American demonstrations.

It was the burning at the stake of a Mexican by an infuriated Texan mob. The man had been guilty of an atrocious crime, but he was denied the trial to which laws and treaty stipulations entitled him. The manner of his execution was infamous. We affect to look down upon Mexicans who tolerate the brutality of bullfights, but when it comes to downright savagery Americans out-do them.

If white Americans were to be burned at the stake by "Greasers" a roar of indignation would sweep over the country from the Rio Grande to the St. Johns. If there were any Mexican handy, they would be mobbed. What would we do, Mexicans have done.

This country is not is not in a position to assume an ultra virtuous tone when it comes to discussing mobs. American mobs have murdered Italians, Chinamen, and Mexicans, and the guilty parties have escaped because state justice would not touch them, and federal justice could not reach them. Take the case of the Mexican lynched in Texas. The men who killed him should be punished, but if the Mexican government were to ask that it be done, the national government would have to say that it could do no more than ask the Texas authorities to do their duty—which they would not.

Surely it is time to enact the legislation first urged by President Harrison, making offenses against the treaty rights of foreigners domiciled in the United States cognizable in the federal courts. Then, when a foreigner was lynched in Louisiana or Idaho the United States government could do something besides expressing regret and paying an indemnity.

WASHINGTON POST
January 30, 1911

WOMEN JOIN LYNCHERS. CLERGYMEN ALSO IN MOB THAT HANGS LOUISIANA NEGRO.

[Special to The Washington Post.]
NEW ORLEANS, January 29.—Aroused by an attack upon the little daughter of Henry Miller, a sawmill owner, a mob of men and women of St. Tammany Parish yesterday and hanged "Wash," a negro who has been employed by the Miller family since his boyhood. Several clergymen, it is said, also were numbered among the lynchers, who intercepted deputy sheriffs who had started for Covington with the negro.

Yesterday morning, Mr. Miller went to his sawmill and Mrs. Miller went to visit neighbors, leaving their little daughter in charge of the negro. When Mrs. Miller returned, "Wash" was gone and the little girl, badly injured, told of the attack. The negro was found cowering in a hayloft.

ATLANTA CONSTITUTION
February 17, 1911

NEGRO MOB GUARDED AND SAVED PRISONERS.

STANFORD, Ky., February 16.—A mob or negroes, heavily armed, stood on guard outside the jail here last night prepared to resist any attempt of a white mob to lynch the blacks, Louis Gregory and Curley Johnson, held for the robbery of three white tobacco farmers of the Danville pike last Monday night.

It is believed the action of the negro mob, had the effect of warding off an attempt to lynch the prisoners. At midnight a posse of armed white men, who are neighbors of the highwaymen's victims, drove into town and scouted the jail. They advised against an attempt to storm the jail. It is believed, because the slightest movement against the negro prisoners would have resulted in a fierce class between the races.

Sheriff McCarthy and a squad of deputies stood guard in front of the jail during the night. They paid no attention to the negroes demonstration, although several shots were fired in the blacks' camp. There is bitter feeling against the negroes in this vicinity. Whites are going armed.

NEW YORK TIMES

April 21, 1911

LYNCHED ON OPERA HOUSE STAGE.

CALHOUN, Ky., April 20.—The little opera house at Livermore, eight miles from here, never witnessed such a melodrama as was staged tonight when Will Potter, a negro, was dragged before the footlights and his body riddled with bullets from the guns of an audience of 50 determined avengers. Of about 200 shots fired, nearly half entered the body of the black man and the remainder torn to shreds the woodland scenery arranged for the presentation of a much milder drama.

While the mob was doing its work in the playhouse, Frank Mitchell, white (22 years old), lay dying at the home of his father from a bullet wound in his chest inflicted by the negro, the shot piercing one of his lungs. At a late hour physicians held out no hope of his recovery.

The drama that had such an ending started with an argument in a poolroom between Mitchell, who is the son of William Mitchell, a liveryman and prominent citizen of the little town, and the negro Potter. Exactly what the men quarreled about has not been definitely established, but it is aid that Potter drew a gun and threatened to kill Mitchell if he did not immediately leave the poolroom. Mitchell is said to have backed out of the place, and when he reached the street to have addressed some remark to Potter. He then hurried up the street.

The white man was only a short distance from the poolroom when Potter ran after him and without warning shot him. As Mitchell fell, Potter turned and ran. He was captured with a few minutes by City Marshal V.P. Stabler, and taken to the lockup. When the news of the shooting spread through the town the citizens became infuriated, and a mob was organized with the avowed intention of lynching the negro. Hearing of the intended assault on the lockup, which is a flimsy structure, the Marshal hastily swore in a half dozen Deputies and took his trembling prisoner to the Opera House. All the doors were bolted and the prisoner was hidden in the basement beneath the stage.

Then the Marshal began preparations to receive the mob, having first telephones to Sheriff T.E. Beeler at Calhoun to come immediately to his assistance with a posse. Before he could fortify his stronghold, however, the mob appeared and demanded the surrender of the negro. Failing to get a ready answer from the little force in the Opera House, the 50 men in the streets made a combined assault on the front doors, and within a few minutes had overpowered the Marshal and his deputies. A search was then made for the negro, who was finally dragged from underneath the stage, shivering with terror.

After a short consultation he was dragged before the footlights and tied. His captors then ranged themselves in the orchestra pit, and at a given signal began to shoot. For a minute or more the auditorium reverberated with the roar of the pistols and rifles, and then all was still. Leaving the negro where he lay, a limp and bloody bundle, the mob filed out into the streets, and in a few minutes had dispersed.

The shooting of the negro was done in a weird scene. Against the wall props, long unused, were bare windows, and startled from their night's rest, rats scurried across the floor. Against such a background the negro was bound hand and foot and placed in the centre of the stage. Many of the lights when the current was turned on refused to burn, and in the semi-darkness, the mob silhouetted against the theatre walls, awaited the signal of their leader. When it was given 50 guns the mob fired in unison, one piercing scream was heard, and their work was over. The lights were then extinguished, the curtain lowered, and the mob then filed out.

WASHINGTON BEE
May 6, 1911

A NEGRO EDITOR CONDEMNS KENTUCKY'S

LATEST BARBARITY. THE WHITE PRESS AND PULPIT STRANGELY SILENT.

To the Editor of the Bee: As a member of the Negro race, and knowing you as I do, I ask that you give me space in your valuable paper, which is largely read by both races, to say a few words anent the treatment of Negroes in this country, but more especially to those poor and unfortunate Negroes who are residing in the Southland. You, reserving the right as what should or should not be published in your paper, I trust that you will see your way clear and publish same for me.

To begin with, I desire to call the attention of your readers to the special telegraphic dispatch from Kentucky to the Washington Post of April 20, 1911, which reads as follows:

"Louisville, Ky., April 20. Kentucky established a new record in lynching today, when a mob in Livermore took M. Potter, a Negro, who had killed a white man, from jail, hanged him on the stage of the local opera house, and charged admission for persons to enter and shoot at the body hanging above the footlights.

"It is reported that the money taken in at the door went to the family of the white man the Negro had killed. Those who bought orchestra seats had the privilege of emptying their six-shooters at the swaying form above them, but gallery occupants were limited to one shot. The whole town is reported still in possession of the mob."

Gentle reader, the lynching is bad enough, but when a set of white barbarians, after lynching a man who was in chains in the jail, in consequence of which was defenseless, and then after killing him in such an unmerciful manner, charge admission fees for the purpose of gazing on their foul deed. and gave the receipt to the family of the dead man, is indeed beyond all human civilization. It is worse than anytime preceding the Christian era. It is shocking. Barbarism pales into insignificance, and the civilized world stands aghast with such a crime.

The killing or lynching of the Negro Potter is the most brutal, the most dastardly, the most fiendish act that could be perpetrated upon any human being, least of all upon the body of a dead man, who was lynched by a set of white marauders, who constitute judges and jurors, wherever there is an alleged crime committed by Negroes. But this time the poor Negro did not commit the nameless crime, which has always suspended him in the air, whether he is guilty or not guilty, and which is always used as sign for wholesale butchery of Negroes.

The crime, of course, is an abominable one when perpetrated, and tends to anger both white and black people, and no man abominates that crime more than the man who now writes this article. But it proves conclusively this time that—this is not the only offense that he is subjected to pay a death penalty.

To talk of the Dark Continent; to talk of sending missionaries to forcign lads for the purpose of civilizing and Christianizing others; is such a mockery of Christianity that I fail to understand why such a farce is not stopped.

Now, where is civilization? Where is religion? Where is law? Where is right? Where is humanity? Is the grand old Commonwealth verging towards barbarism, savagery, and cultism? Where in the world is the commonwealth? Where are its laws? Where are the conservators of the peace? Where is Christianity? Has justice fled from the bosom of the white people in Kentucky? I hope not.

This atrocious deed, which is a blot on the fair State, was perpetuated upon the defenseless Negro, not because he was charged with having committed rape, for, indeed, when such a cry is made, it not only stirs the white people of the country, but the Negroes, too, feel it as keenly, as much as any other human being, and there are instances where Negroes have given their aid in hunting down reckless and abominable men who have robbed women of their virtue. But it happened that this is the mere killing of a white man, who no doubt had brought it upon himself by his overbearing manner, as is usually the case when a Negro kills a white man.

This question of revenge and cruelty is not one of sentiment, nor one for mawkish oratory, but is a question that goes to the very foundation of the well-being of human society, and concerns the humanizing social, moral, and civil salvation, elevation, and evolution of the best gifts, graces, accomplishments of that portion of the human family. Who for centuries have been denuded of all human rights, civil and political privileges by their cousins and half-brothers and sisters of the sons of Shem and Japhet. Who for centuries arrogated to themselves all the rights and privileges of the highest forms of modern civilization based upon Christianity.

But, after all, their boasted civilization does not make them better citizens that the poor Negro who has had no civilization, according to the white man's idea of civilization.

Many Negroes have been lynched without the least provocation, although it is said that we are living in a Christian land. In conclusion, let me say that the white man has not done his duty in way of protecting the Negroes in this country.

Yours for the race,
W.D. JOHNSON,
Former Editor of the *Kentucky Standard.*

COLORADO SPRINGS GAZETTE
May 30, 1911

MEXICAN LYNCHED FOR SHOUTING "VIVA DIAZ"

EL PASO, May 29.—A special to the *Times* from Barstow, Ward County, Texas, reported the lynching of a Mexican whose name in unknown, for shouting "Viva Diaz." The Mexican was surrounded by a crowd of American-Mexicans and shot to death. The incident happened while the American-Mexicans were celebrating the success of Madero. No arrests have been made.

WASHINGTON POST
June 2, 1911

APPLAUD COLORED LYNCHERS. WHITE MEN CHEER AS MOB SEIZES NEGRO CRITIC OF SLAVE OWNERS.

[Special to the Washington Post]
JACKSON, Miss., June 1.—With white men applauding their efforts, a mob composed entirely of negroes, stormed the jail and lynched Alfred Johnson, near Shelby Miss., for killing "Hamp" Moore, an aged negro.

The killing followed an argument, in which Moore

reprimanded the younger negro for bitter words denouncing Southern slave owners among the white race during the times antedating the civil war.

NORFOLK WEEKLY NEWS JOURNAL
June 30, 1911

WARRANTS ISSUED FOR THE LYNCHING OF A MEXICAN.

CAMERON, Texas, June 23.—Warrants have been issued for four persons suspected of having participated in the lynching of a Mexican boy at Thorndale, near here, several days ago. More warrants are probable. The names have not been made public.

MANSFIELD (OHIO) NEWS
August 16, 1911
RACE RIOT IN TEXAS.
GALVESTON, Tex., Aug. 16.—Several persons were injured in a race riot at Jourdanton, Atascosa County, between Americans and Mexicans. First, a Mexican was lynched by Americans for complicity in the murder of an American officer. Then, when officers arrested another Mexican on the same charge, rival mobs of Americans and Mexicans sought to take the prisoner from the officers. However, while they were fighting in form of the jail, the Mexican was spirited away. Further trouble is expected.

MAHONING DISPATCH (CANFIELD, OHIO)
August 25, 1911

ALLEGED LYNCHER CLEARED.

CALHOUN, KY., Aug. 23.—Lawrence Mitchell, alleged leader of the mob that lynched William Potter, a negro, in the opera house at Livermore, was acquitted by the jury which is trying the lynching cases. It is believed that the other alleged members of the mob will also be cleared.

MIDDLETOWN DAILY TIMES PRESS
February 5, 1912

CREMATE LYNCHED NEGRO. GEORGIA MOB NOT SATISFIED WITH FIRST VENGEANCE.

MACON, Ga., Feb. 5.—The body of Charles Powell, the negro who was lynched for criminal assault on a white girl, was burned by the mob here. The body of the negro was taken from an undertaking establishment, where it had been pace on exhibition, and was carried to a field in South Macon, in the midst of a populous negro settlement, and cremated.

The body was placed in a delivery wagon, which was followed through the streets for over a mile by a crowd of over 500 men and boys, who shouted, "Save the count money!"

EVENING POST (FREDERICK, MARYLAND)
February 26, 1912

ALLEGED LYNCHERS ON TRIAL.

GEORGETOWN, Texas. Feb. 26.—Ezra W. Stephens, Harry Wuenske, and G.F. Noack, three residents of Milan County, were arraigned in the district court here today to answer to a charge of murder in the first degree as the result of their alleged participation in the lynching of Antonio Gomez, at Thorndale last June. Gomez, a young Mexican, was lynched after he had stabbed Charles Z. Shank to death.

ATLANTA CONSTITUTION
September 2, 1913

CASE OF LIGE LANE.

In the case of the negro sentenced to death for the commission of a criminal assault on a white woman, a commutation of sentence is urged by the judge who tried the case, the solicitor general, and the woman on whom the assault is said to have been committed. It is urged that the evidence was insufficient to convict, and that the woman in the case is of notoriously bad character, and is now under indictment for selling whisky.

NAUGATUCK (CT) DAILY NEWS

September 2, 1913

WHITE WOMEN WOULD SAVE NEGRO FROM HANGING. ALLEGED VICTIM URGES GOVERNOR TO COMMUTE SENTENCE.

ATLANTA, Ga., Sept. 2.—For the first time known in the history of the State Prison Commission, a large number of well-known white women have recommended executive clemency for a negro charged with an offense against a white woman.

Lige Lane was convicted in Clinch County for assault. He was sentenced to hang and unless the governor interferes will be hanged on September 10. Attorney R.G. Dickerson appearing before the State Prison Commission yesterday and urged that it recommended a commutation of Lane's sentence to life imprisonment. He said there were grave doubts as to the guilt of Lane.

Supporting his application, Attorney Dickerson submitted petitions signed by 95 percent of the white women of Homerville, and 90 percent of the registered voters of that town, as well as letters from the judge and solicitor who tried the negro, and many county officials. A letter written by the negro's alleged victim, which also requests clemency was submitted.

ATLANTA CONSTITUTION

September 10, 1913

LIGE LANE'S SENTENCE COMMUTED BY

SLATON. NEGRO CONDEMNED TO DIE SPARED ON PLEAS OF CLINCH COUNTY CITIZENS.

Among the last things done by Governor Slaton, just before he left his office Tuesday afternoon was to save the life of a negro named Lige Lane, who was sentenced to hang today in Clinch County for committing an assault on a white woman.

The governor acted on the recommendation of the Prison Commission, who asked that mercy be extended, and also on the petition of the trial judge and solicitor and the clerk of court, who certified that they represented at least 90 percent of the sentiment of the white people in the county in which the conviction had been obtained, in holding that it was unwarranted on account of the notorious bad character of the complainant.

As soon as the order granting the commutation of sentence was signed, it was transmitted to the Prison Commission with instructions to notify the sheriff at once, so that the hanging might not take place. In connection with his granting the order of commutation, the governor issued the following signed statement, explanatory of his act.

Statement

By the Governor.

"This application for commutation from a death sentence to imprisonment for life of a negro convicted of assaulting a white woman is remarkable. The evidence, if credible, warrants the verdict.

The woman was a depraved character, who, the evidence shows, by her improper relations, separated a negro from his wife. Her business was that of unlawfully selling liquor. When the offense was committed, she did not know the name of the assailant, although she must have known Lige Lane, the defendant, who owed her a nay for some corn liquor. Her son, to whom she told the circumstances, asked the deputy sheriff to arrest another negro as the offender.

When Lane was arrested on Monday morning after the previous Saturday night on which the offense was committed, he was at work on the outskirts of Homerville, the scene of the crime. Ninety percent of the white women of Homerville, as certified to me officially by the clerk or the superior court, the judge, and the solicitor general who tried the case, and the woman for assaulting, who Lige Lane is under sentence of death, request me to commute the sentence. The Prison Commission unanimously recommends it.

I cannot claim to esteem the virtue and the safety of the women of Clinch County more than those who have urged upon me the exercise of clemency. The negro is friendless and without money. It is not a case of power and influence. The recommendation of the Prison Commission is approved, and the sentence of Lige Lane is commuted to life imprisonment."

(Signed) JOHN M. SLATON, "GOVERNOR"

Bob Dickson, an attorney from Homerville, made an argument to the governor to spare the life of the negro.

WASHINGTON POST
January 28, 1914

WOMEN LYNCH SLAYER. MOB OF BOTH SEXES HANGS NEGRO.

RALEIGH, N.C. Jan. 27.—Having confessed, it is alleged, that he had attacked and killed Mrs. William Lynch, wife of a well-known Johnson County farmer, James Wilson, a negro was lynched by a mob this afternoon near the scene of his alleged crime. The lynching took place while a company of militia was hurrying from Raleigh in automobiles to protect the negro.

Suspicion having fallen upon Wilson, he was arrested last night near Selma, N.C. He is said to have made a partial confession this morning, and a crowd demanded that he be taken to the scene of the crime. Hoping to avert mob violence, the officers took refuge with their prisoner in a store, and telephoned Gov. Craig for aid. Soon a crowd of nearly 1,000 men and women gathered about the store, overpowered the officers, dragged the negro out, and swung him from a tree limb. Making sign he wanted to speak, he was let down, and implicated another negro name Saunders, now under arrest at Wendell. He was swung up again, and his body riddled with bullets.

Mrs. Lynch's body was found covered with underbrush near the house by her husband when he got home, Saturday night from a short trip.

NEW YORK TIMES
April 5, 1914

"LYNCH LAW"

[To the Editor of The *New York Times:*]

In regards to your dispatch from Wagner, Okla., stating that a certain negress had been lynched in that section because she had stabbed one of a party of young white men, who were visiting the negro section. Permit me to inquire whether, if the case had been reversed, would a lynching have taken place? To my dull mind a murder is a murder, no matter by what hand committed; the punishment, whether by law or mob-"law," should be the same, whether the hand that strikes the fatal blow be dark-skinned or light-skinned.

If a party of young colored men were to visit the white section in some place in Oklahoma, and one of these colored men were stabbed to death by a white woman, would the lynching of the latter be any less justified than that of the negress reported?

H.G.K.
New York, April 3, 1914.

NEW YORK TIMES
July 13, 1914

MOB LYNCHES NEGRO WOMAN.

ORANGEBURG, S.C. July 12.—Rosa Carson, a negro woman, was taken from the jail at Elloree near her, today, and lynched by a mob. She is said to have confessed to beating to death the 12-year-old daughter r of D.F. Bell yesterday.

VAN WERT DAILY BULLETIN
December 24, 1914

MEXICAN LYNCHED. COWBOYS SHOOT TO DEATH ALLEGED MURDERER OF A JAILER.

Oakville, Texas, December 24.—A mob of cowboys lynched Isidro Gonzales, a Mexican, who is alleged to have chocked Harry Hinton, county jailer here, to death last Sunday night, and then escaped from jail. The lynching occurred near the town, the body of the lynched Mexican victim was riddled with bullets.

NEW YORK TIMES
January 16, 1915

WHOLE FAMILY LYNCHED.

ATLANTA, Ga., Jan. 15.—Dan Barber, his son Jesse, and two married daughters, Bula and Ella Charles, negroes, were taken from the Jasper County Jail at Monticello, Georgia, last night by a mob and lynched.

The lynchings resulted indirectly from a fight that recently occurred at Dan Barber's home, when J.P. Williams, Chief of Police, attempted to arrest him on a charge of selling whisky without a license. Barber appeared to have peaceably surrendered, when he suddenly seized a revolver, and opened fire on the officer. Barber's son, Jesse, and the two Charles women then joined in an attack upon the policeman, beating him severely. Negroes living nearby noticed the county authorities, and the four were placed in jail.

Late last night, according to Sheriff Ezell, a mob of 100 white men entered the jail, overpowered him, took his keys, unlocked the cells, and took the negroes from the building. The negroes were lynched one at a time, being first hanged, then shot. Their bodies, riddled with bullets, were found on the outskirts of town today.

WASHINGTON POST

July 31, 1915

BURNED AT THE STAKE. TEXAS MOB LYNCHES COLORED MAN HELD AS CHILDREN'S SLAYER. WOMEN AND GIRLS PRESENT.

Temple. Tex. July 30.—Will Stanley, Colored, arrested today on a charge of murdering three children of W. R. Grimes, a farmer, near Temple, Wednesday, was taken from the justice courtroom, and burned to death by a mob in the public square here late tonight. Several thousand men and women, who thronged the streets awaiting the outcome of an examination of Stanley and two alleged accomplices, witnessed the lynching.

Cheers About Pyre.

The scene on the well-lighted public square at the time of the burning of Stanley was spectacular. The mob had chosen an open space in which to build their pyre, this being surrounded by men who yelled and cheered as they shoved the prisoner into the flames. All about the streets were filled with pedestrians and automobiles loaded with onlookers. Trees fringing the street on the side of the square nearest the burning were filled with boys, while scattered through the crowds were many young girls.

Shoved Back Into Flames.

When Stanley was cast into the flames he struggled to escape, but was repeatedly shoved back. Several men said Stanley confessed that he did the killing, claiming that he had been hired to do the deed. He begged to be permitted to live long enough to tell about it, but his alleged admission of guilt was sufficient for those around the fire. A shot was fired, which some claim struck the struggling man. His struggles soon ceased, and the crowd began to disperse.

Leo M. Frank, the superintendent of a pencil factory in Marietta, was accused of raping and murdering Mary Phagan, his thirteen-year-old employee. He was convicted of the murder, but his sentence was commuted to life in prison. A lynch mob kidnapped and killed him on August 17, 1915. The back of this photograph says, "J. L. Sibley, Marietta, Ga."

Leo M. frank.

The body of Leo Frank, hanging from an oak tree on August 16, 1915

Leo Frank's alleged victim; Mary Phagan's clothes and the rope used to kill her.

OAKLAND (CA) TRIBUNE
January 23, 1916

A LETTER ON LYNCHING.

The university commission on Southern race questions at its session in Durham, N.C., issued a statement on the subject of lynching to college men of the South. From it, we learn that "lynching is a contagious social disease." Perhaps this is so. Certainly, the quoted term is one, which might by ingenious argument be made to include a multitude of sins. Many of us have, however, preferred to isolate each case for analysis and try to excuse it on the ground that suddenly outraged and infuriated citizens, impatient at the tedious and uncertain devices of legal justice, mixed with the avenging spirit and the desire to provide a more effective object lesson in fatal proportions.

It has not always been easy to justify lynching on these grounds, but just as many exceptions arise under the theory of contagious social disease. In the figures of lynching compiled for 1914, how shall we classify the lynching of a man for being found under a house? Of a man for assisting a man who had wounded another to escape, and of one for stealing shoes?

If the explanation of the university commission is correct, the disease is spreading, and is intensified by much less serious offenses than formerly. Until recent years, murder and rape were almost the sole crimes calling for "lynch justice." The increase in 1915 over the previous year was 30 percent. Four victims were later discovered to have been innocent of the crime for which lynched. The letter closes with this statement:

> "These are the terrible facts. It there no remedy? Have we not sufficient legal intelligence and machinery to take care of every case of crime committed? Must we fall back on the methods of the jungle? Civilization rests on obedience of law, which means the substitution of reason and deliberation for impulse, instinct, and passion. It is easy and tempting to obey the latter, but to be

> governed by the former requires self-control, which comes from the interposition of thought between impulse and action. Herein lies the college men's opportunity to serve his fellows, to interpose deliberation between impulses and action, and in that way to control both."

This is a worthy undertaking, and the college men will no doubt exert a good influence. They realize, as well as any one, however, that deliberation between impulse and action is not always and effective antidote to the "disease." There never was a case that afforded fuller opportunity for deliberation than that of Leo M. Frank of Georgia. Judging from the sources whence came praise for the mob that invaded the penitentiary to take Frank to the tree, college men are not always immune from the social disorder of the South.

Birth of A Nation. **The film premiered on February 8, 1915**

A quote from Woodrow Wilson used in the film *Birth of A Nation*. The film premiered on February 8, 1915, at Clune's Auditorium in downtown Los Angeles. Furthermore, "*The Birth of a Nation* (premiered with the title The Clansman) is a 1915 silent film directed by D. W. Griffith. Set during and after the American Civil War, the film was based on Thomas Dixon's The Clansman, a novel and play. The Birth of a Nation is noted for its innovative camera techniques and narrative achievements, and its status as the first Hollywood "blockbuster." It has provoked great controversy for promoting white supremacy, and positively portraying the Ku Klux Klan as heroes."[4]

---

[4] MJ Movie Reviews - The Birth of a Nation, (1915), by Dan DeVore, (January 23, 2003).

Lynching of Jesse Washington, Waco, Texas. May 15, 1916.

NEW YORK TIMES
May 16, 1916

15,000 WITNESS LYNCHING IN TEXAS. CHARRED BODY IS PLACED IN SACK & HUNG ON TELEPHONE POLE.

WACO, Texas, May 15.—With 15.000 persons as witnesses, including women and children, Jesse Washington, a negro boy, who confessed that he had criminally assaulted and murdered Mrs. Lucy Fryer seven miles south of here last Monday afternoon, was taken from the Fifth District Courtroom shortly before noon today, and burned to death on the public square.

The burning came immediately after the negro's trial had ended. The jury-had returned a verdict of guilty. Then someone started the cry of "Get the negro." It was quickly taken up by all the spectators in the courtroom, and Washington was seized.

The mob at first intended to hang the negro from the suspension bridge, but a suggestion that he be burned on the plaza met with approval. The prisoner was dragged to the City Hall yard, where the chain already around his neck was thrown over the limb of a tree. Wood was piled around him and the fire started.

The rush for the negro came so suddenly that officers, lawyers, and newspapermen were swept off their feet. About 1 o'clock members of the mob returned to the scene, put the charred body into a sack, and a man on horseback dragged the body through the main streets. The horseman headed in the direction of Robinson, where Mrs. Fryer was murdered. At Robinson the sack was suspended from a telephone pole, where it remained for several hours.

GETTYSBURG (PA) TIMES
June 21, 1916

MEXICAN LYNCHED BY TEXANS.

BROWNWOOD, Tex., June 21.—Geronimo Lerma, a Mexican, suspected of attacking Mrs. W.U. Kuykendall while she slept, was found later by a posse about ten miles from here, and shot to death.

NEW YORK TIMES
October 5, 1916

LYNCH WOMAN IN GEORGIA. RIDDLES THE BODY WITH BULLETS.

ALBANY, Ga., Oct.—A negro woman named Connelly, whose son is charged with killing a white farmer after a quarrel, in which she took part, was taken from jail at Leary, Ga., on Monday night and lynched, according to reports reaching here today. Her body was found yesterday riddled with bullets. The son is under arrest.

WASHINGTON POST
December 3, 1917

THOUSANDS LOOK ON AS NEGRO IS BURNED.

NASHVILLE, Tenn., Dec. 2.—A dispatch from Dyersburg, Tenn., tonight says Ligon Scott, a negro who is alleged to have criminally assaulted a white woman in Dyer County, November 22, was burned at the stake on the public square there today. Scott was arrested in Jackson, Tenn., Saturday and was being brought to Dyersburg in an automobile by the sheriff and his deputies when a mob met the officers and relieved them of their prisoners.

The entire county soon knew of the capture, and thousands flocked to town. The negro confessed his guilt and was taken to a vacant lot at the public square. An iron stake was driven in the ground and the negro was tied to this. He was then stripped of his clothing and a bonfire was lighted. His body was soon consumed by the flames.

The crowd was orderly, and carried out the execution without a hitch. The members dispersed before night and the usual Sunday quietude reigns in the city tonight.

NEW YORK TRIBUNE
August 5, 1918

TWO MEN NAMED AS LEADERS OF GEORGIA MOB BY WORKER.

Walter F. White, assistant secretary of the National Association for the Advancement of Colored People, has identified two ringleaders and fifteen other members of the recent negro lynching mobs in Brooks and Lowndes Counties, Georgia, according to an announcement made yesterday by John R. Shillady, secretary of the association. Mr. White, he said, had given the names of seventeen men to Governor Dorsey of Georgia, with a complete report of his investigation.

It was discovered, Mr. Shillady said, that instead of the six lynchings reported in the district in newspapers last May, there were eleven, all the result of the killing of Hampton Smith, a white man, and the wounding of his wife on May 16.

Eleven negroes had died at the hands of mobs by May 22.

Mr. White's report was given to Governor Dorsey on July 10 and a few days ago a copy was sent to President Wilson.

BILLINGS (MONTANA) GAZETTE
July 20, 1919

SOUTHERN LYNCHINGS.

It is a manifest duty of congress to conduct a searching investigation into southern lynchings. This paper, in common with other publications of the country, has been made the recipient of a circular letter issued by the National Association for the Advancement of Colored People, wherein is reproduced an item in the Jackson, Miss., Daily News of Thursday, June 26, 1919.

The item is "played up," to us a newspaper expression, with a two-column head, and calmly announced that John Hartfield will be lynched that afternoon at 5 o'clock. The "deck" in the head states that Governor Bilbo admits he is powerless to prevent the lynching, as are the authorities and sheriff. Thousands of people are flocking to Ellisville to attend the event according to the *Jackson Daily*.

Governor Bilbo is quoted to this effect: "The state has no troops, and if the civil authorities at Ellisville are helpless, the state is equally so. Furthermore, excitement is at such a high pitch throughout Mississippi that any armed attempt to interfere with the mob would doubtless result in the death of hundreds of persons."

It would appear that mob murders are advertised in the press of Mississippi, Louisiana, and other states, and that state officials have confessed their inability to accord citizens of the United States the protection guaranteed under the constitution. Admittedly there are cases where bestiality has been so pronounced that mob law appeals to many persons, but such performances only redound to the discredit of the state where committed.

Conviction in duly constituted courts would almost invariably follow, and the commonwealth would thus be relieved of the stigma attaching to its name. Justice would have its dues by the regular process just as effectually as it seeks to obtain it by overriding the law. Congress should take immediate action on the anti-lynching bill now pending.

NEW YORK TIMES
July 25, 1919

LYNCHING KEPT SECRET. GEORGIA NEGRO'S CRIME WAS DEFENDING NEGRESS AGAINST WHITE MAN.

ATLANTA, Ga., July 24.—Berry Washington, a 72-year-old negro, was lynched near Milan, Ga., on May 26, for killing a white man in defense of a negro woman. This information is contained in a story, which *The Atlanta Constitution* will publish tomorrow. Officials of Milan, the story says, declared at the time that they wished to keep news of the affair from becoming public in order to assist them in arresting the lynchers, but according to the account no arrests have been made.

NEW YORK TRIBUNE
August 19, 1918

A PRICE ON LYNCHERS. AN EXTRAORDINARY ANNOUNCEMENT BY THE SAN ANTONIO EXPRESS.

The publishers of *The San Antonio Express* have established and set aside a fund of $100,000 to be used in combating the crime of lynching in this country, thereby to aid in stamping out the lawlessness and violence of the mob. At the latest meeting of the stockholders of the Express Publishing Company, August 1, it was determined to devote this sum of money to the purpose of rewarding persons who shall be directly responsible for the arrest and conviction of those who incite riots and mob outbreaks that result in lynching, and of those who perpetrate the lynching crime itself.

It was the earnest, expressed opinion of every member of the stockholding body at the meeting that the irremediable injustices, the debasement and degradation worked by a crime that invariably exhibits contempt for law and order, and an enmity to decent systems of courts and law enforcement, must be brought to an end throughout the United States. Lynching must no longer go unpunished or lightly punished, in any state or districts of this nation.

Lynchers of Negroes Especially.

The anti-lynching fund of The San Antonio Express will be employed in this manner: **A reward of $500** will be paid to each person who shall be directly responsible for the arrest with subsequent conviction and punishment of any person or persons who were instrumental in arousing a mob to commit a lynching or in putting through the lynching itself, when the individual lynched **was not a negro**.

A reward of $1000 will be paid to each person who shall be directly responsible for the arrest, with subsequent conviction and punishment, of any person or persons who were instrumental in arousing a mob to commit a lynching or in putting through the lynching itself, **when the individual was a negro**. This fund of $1000, 000 and the offer of reward there under will be maintained and in effect for a period of five years from August 3, 1918. The system of rewards will apply to any and every crime of lynching committed with the bounds of Continental United States that is, exclusive of the American possessions of Puerto Rico, Hawaii, the Philippine Islands, the Panama Canal Zone, ect.

Rewards Open To Everybody.

These rewards will be paid to private citizens of either sex or to peace officers of whatever class. Sheriff, their deputies, and possemen; constables and their deputies; United States Marshals, their deputies and possemen; city or state police, rangers, ect.; officers and men of the organized military forces or National Guard of the several states, and to any and all other persons who may not be debarred legally from the acceptance of a reward for this character of law enforcement.

Lynching of Whites Is Rare.

As compared with the number of instances of such outrages against negroes and against the law, the decency, and the morality of the people—instances of the lynching of whites are rare.

It must be noted that payment of these rewards. It must be noted that payment of these rewards is strictly conditioned upon not only the arrest but also the conviction and punishment by court or jury, according to the system that may obtain in the jurisdiction wherein the crime was committed of the lynchers. Only by stringent punishment may this destructive crime be kept down and finally eradicated.

Those entrusted with the use of "The Express" anti-lynching fund will have nothing to do with cases in which conviction is followed by suspended sentence, or by any punishment that does not fit the crime; that is, there must be the death penalty or a term of years in the state's prison, according to the circumstances of the crime in evidence.

Whenever claim shall be made for the payment of reward out of this fund, the management of "The Express" will investigate fully as to the criminal's connection with the arrest and trial of the lyncher, whether the lyncher's conviction and punishment were effected through genuine interest of the claimant, by information to the authorities and by honest testimony in court. Further details as to the operation on this system of rewards may be announced at some future date.

A Fight For Self-Respect

The creation of this fund was voted by the stockholders on the recommendation of George W. Brackenridge, of San Antonio. Mr. Brackenridge has been energetically and practically interested for years in the various efforts of both legal authority and social throughout the Union to do away with mob violence, especially when it takes the form of lynching.

"*The San Antonio Express*, like most other self-respecting newspapers on either side of Mason and Dixon's Line, has for years made a vigorous fight editorially against a condition of lawlessness and brutality that blackens the name and damages the citizenship of any community, South or North, that witnesses, and allows a single lynching.

Public sentiment against this crime is steadily gaining strength, in the number of adherents pledged to law and order, and in stern expressions by assemblies of good citizens everywhere in the United States"

NEW YORK TIMES
September 1, 1919

EX-NEGRO SOLDIER WHO ATTACKED WHITE WOMAN IS HUNG AND BURNED.

BOGALUSA, La., Aug. 31.—After being trailed by bloodhounds, caught, and identified by a white woman as the man who attacked her Saturday, Lucius McCarty, a discharged negro soldier, was lynched here today by a mob of more than 1,000 men.

His body was then tied to an automobile, dragged through the principal streets of the town, and finally burned in front of the home of his victim.

MAHONING COUNTY (OHIO) DISPATCH
October 3, 1919

DOMESTIC LYNCHING NEWS.

OMAHA, Neb., is again quiet following the rioting which resulted in the injury to the mayor, the lynching of William Brown, a negro, accused of recently attacking Miss Agnes Lobeck, a white girl. The death of one white man, the injury to several scores of whites and negroes, and the partial destruction of the new $1, 5000,000 county courthouse, which was set on fire by members of the mob. With federal troops patrolling the streets it was believed that the authorities would be able to prevent any possible fresh disorders, which began when a mob set out to lynch Brown. Maj. Gen. Leonard Wood has taken charge of military operations.

Will Brown, lynched and burned in the Omaha, Nebraska Riot of 1919.

The burning of Will Brown's body, Omaha, Nebraska, Sept. 28

Postcard depicting the lynching of Lige Daniels, Center, Texas, USA, August 3, 1920. The back reads, "He killed Earl's grandma.

She was Florence's mother. Give this to Bud. From Aunt Myrtle."

NEW YORK TIMES
August 3, 1920

TEXAS MOB LYNCHED NEGRO IN JAIL YARD.

CENTER, Texas, Aug. 2.—A mob of more than 1,000 men this afternoon stormed the county jail, battered down the steel doors, wrecked the steel cell and took out Lige Daniels, negro, charged with the murder of a white woman, and hanged him to a limb of an oak tree in the courthouse yard.

The lynching followed announcement by authorities of a full confession made to the Grand Jury now in session, and the District Attorney. The wife of a well-known farmer living near Center was brutally attacked and later found unconscious at a lonely pond near her home last Thursday night. Her skull was crushed and her body was bruised and lacerated. She was brought to a local sanitarium, where she died Friday.

Captain W.A. Bridges, commanding Company L, 7th Cavalry, received instructions from Austin to protect the prisoner and to prevent the lynching, but he was unable to find any member of his company in time. Shortly after the lynching, the crowd dispersed and the town quickly resumed its normal appearance.

CEDAR RAPIDS (IOWA) EVENING GAZETTE
January 27, 1921

TOWN QUIET AFTER NEGRO BURNING.

WILSON, Ark., Jan. 27.—Reports from Nodena near the scene of the lynching last night of Henry Lowry, Negro, for the killing of O.T. Craig, a planter, and his daughter, Mrs. C.C. Williamson, indicated that conditions in that neighborhood had quieted, and no further disorder was expected.

Telephone messaged from Blytheville and Marion, where several Negroes are in jail charged with having aided Lowry to escape from Arkansas after the killing of Craig and Mrs. Williamson Christmas day also reported the situation quiet and that no attempt had been made to molest the prisoners. Throughout then night rumors were current that mobs were being formed to take the accused Negroes from the Marion and Blytheville jails, but the night passed without disorder.

Lowry was burned to death on the banks of the Mississippi River, about a mile from the Craig plantation, the scene of the killing of the planter and his daughter, who were shot to death when they attempted to quiet Lowry, a tenant farmer, who was creating a disturbance on the Craig plantation. Lowry was brought back to the scene of the crime in an automobile by a party of about a dozen men, who seized him aboard a railroad train at Sardis, Miss., yesterday morning after overpowering and disarming two deputy sheriffs, who were returning him to Arkansas from El Paso, Texas, where he was captured last Friday.

Lowry was given food, permitted to bid goodbye to his wife and children, and then bound to a log and burned. Before the torch was applied, Lowry is said to have confessed to the double killing.

ANNISTON (ALABAMA) STAR
January 28, 1921

NEGROES HELD FOR MURDER REMOVED FOR SAFEKEEPING.

MEMPHIS, Tenn., Jan. 28.—(United Press).—Four negro men, and a negro woman who were held at Marion, Arkansas, for alleged complicity in aiding the escape of Henry Lowry are today in the Arkansas penitentiary at Little Rock. Two negro men held on a similar charge at Blytheville, Ark., were removed to the jail at Caruthersville, Mo.

Arkansas authorities moved the negroes when it appeared that an effort would be made last night to lynch all seven of them.

The negroes held at Marion were brought to Memphis yesterday afternoon, as a blind, Memphis officials say, and were then put in the baggage car of the night express and rushed back through Marion to Little Rock for safekeeping.

Henry Lowry, the negro, whom the seven held are charged with aiding to escape to El Paso, Texas, after he killed two persons at Nodena, Ark., on Christmas Day, was burned to death at Nodena Wednesday night.

THE NEWARK (OHIO) ADVOCATE
February 8, 1921

SHERIFF FORGETS TO HANG NEGRO SLAYER.

BATON ROUGE, La., Feb. 8.—Sheriff T. A. Grant of Ouachita Parish notified Governor Parker today that he had forgotten to hang Lonnie Eaton, negro, convicted of murder, on February 4, as required by sentence and asked what to do with the prisoner. The governor has put the problem up to Attorney General Coco. Sheriff Grant's letter said he had been so busy with other matters on February 4, that the scheduled hanging had "completely slipped his mind."

WASHINGTON POST
February 9, 1921

FORGETS TO HANG CONDEMNED MAN. SHERIFF'S OMISSION GIVES LOUISIANA OFFICIALS QUEER PROBLEM.

NEW ORLEANS, Feb. 8 (By the Associated Press).—With apparently no precedent to guide him, Attorney General A.V. Coco is tonight trying to determine the legal status of Lonnie Eaton, negro, of Monroe, La., the date of whose execution of February 4 for the murder of a white man was completely forgotten by Sheriff T.A. Grant of Ouachita Parish.

The forgetfulness of the sheriff, who became so engrossed in other matters that he entirely overlooked the scheduled hanging until after the date had passed, has raised one of the most interesting legal questions ever met with in this State. The attorney general frankly admits that he does not know what the negro's status is—whether he is already legally dead in the eyes of the law, and should go free by reason of having his life once placed in jeopardy with the setting of the date of his execution by the governor, or whether the man must yet be executed.

CAPITAL TIMES (MADISON, WISCONSIN)

February 10, 1921

DEAD LEGALLY BUT APPETITE IS GOOD.

BATON ROUGE, La.—Lonnie Eaton, the man the sheriff forgot to hang, may be dead legally. Attorney General Coco admitted today he didn't know; but reports from Ouachita Parish prison where Lonnie has been taking in, legally or illegally, his regular three squares a day ever since his execution was mislaid by Sheriff Grant Feb. 4, do not indicate that his appetite has suffered because of his possible demise.

Sheriff wrote the governor yesterday, that in the press of "civil and criminal matters" he utterly forgot the mandate to put the negro to death on that day. The sheriff did not know what to do about it. He had no warrant to execute his prisoner on any other day and asked for instructions. It was said the "once in jeopardy" principle of law might prevent any execution.

NEW YORK TIMES

February 16, 1921

PRAYER AVERTS LYNCHING.

CLYDE, Ga., Feb 15.—A Negro posse, which came to shoot, remained to pray here last night at their prisoner's call. That ended the plans for a lynching, and Israel Waters, a Negro charged with assaulting a schoolgirl of his own race and captured by a posse of white and Negro residents, went to jail instead.

The whites turned Waters over to the Negroes for punishment following his capture. He said today he had been stood up to be shot when he asked the brethren to pray for him, and the mob changed its mind about the shooting.

NEW YORK TIMES
February 17, 1921

NEGRO BURNED AT STAKE. MOB OF 5,000 STORMS THE JAIL IN CLARKE COUNTY, GA.

ATHENS, Ga., Feb. 16.—A mob of 5,000 persons tonight stormed the Clarke County Jail. After taking John Lee Eberhardt, a negro, charged with the murder of Mrs. Walter Lee of Oconee County from the jail, they burned him to the stake. The mob took the negro from the county jail here after leaders had climbed an elevator shaft to the top floor of the Count Court House, where the jail is located, and burned their way into Eberhardt's cell by applying a blowtorch on the locks.

He was taken by the mob to a field about five miles from Athens, directly opposite of the Lee home, and burned at the stake shortly before midnight, after leaders had publicly debated whether he should be hanged or burned. He died in twenty minutes. Mrs. Lee was killed early today after she had been attacked on entering a barn at the Lee farm. She resisted her assailant and ran back toward her home, but was shot from behind. The contents of a double-barreled shotgun were emptied into her back and head. Passing negroes heard the shots and assisted the woman while the negro made his escape.

WASHINGTON POST
March 21, 1921

NEGRO HANGED BY MOB. KILLED COLORED WOMAN AND WAS HELD FOR MURDER.

HATTIESBURG, Miss., March 20.— Arthur Jennings, negro, held here on a charge of killing a negro woman several days ago, was taken from the county jail early today by a number of armed men, who overpowered the sheriff. At daylight, the negro's body was found hanging in a tree near the city.

Jennings, after a pistol duel with deputy sheriffs, in which he was wounded twice, was captured here last week. County Coroner Hulett empanelled a jury this afternoon and is conducting an investigation.

WASHINGTON POST
April 23, 1921

SAVED FROM NEGRO MOB.

[Special to *The Washington Post*]

DANVILLE, Va., April 22.—Bud Carr, a white man, was arrested by William Hatchett and Ezekiel Slade, both colored, and rescued from a large crowd of angry colored citizens here yesterday, after it is charged he is alleged to have assaulted a 13-year-old colored girl at her home. The girl told the police that the man entered her home where she was alone. When the alarm was given, the colored neighbors gathered around the house. Carr is said to have fled through the back door, and to have leaped over a fence with the colored mob in hot pursuit.

A call for the police was sent, but the two negroes overhauled Carr and were on their way to the police station when an automobile containing officers intercepted them. Carr denies the assault charge and says he went into the house to get a drink of water.

COSHOCTON (OHIO) TRIBUNE
March 26, 1921

AMERICAN DIABOLISM.

WHEN a northerner criticizes a lynching he is commonly told that he does not understand the Negro "problem", and ought not to talk about it. In the south itself humane men and women, who are surely in the majority, seem often to be terrorized by the truculent and perverted few.

How else could one account for such atrocities as the burning of Henry Lowry, whose case is described by William Pickens in the *Nation*? For the paralysis of state and local authorities in the presence of a small group of outlaws, who openly advertised their purpose and who twice passed across the three states of Arkansans, Tennessee, and Mississippi on their way to get the victim and bring him to his death? For the failure of the "best people" of three states to protest against an exhibition of such appalling brutality that it cannot be outdone in the history of any people or tribe, however barbarous, ancient or modern? For the concealment of important facts leading to the crime of which Lowry was accused?

Here was a Negro who had been made, with thousands of his race, the victim of what is still virtually a slave system. When he ventures to complain he is struck and bullied. He becomes embittered, sullen, dangerous (though previously he had been considered by his white neighbors "an honest, hard-working, inoffensive Negro"), and when "Mr. dick" Craig fires at him he has his own revolver ready to fire back, sees red, and, shooting into a group of people, kills a man and a woman. The facts do not extenuate the crime, but they explain it.

The north cannot settle the Negro question, but it is time for the federal government, which represents the civilized opinion of America, to see to it that lynchings, no matter where they occur, are punished as other murders are punished. The federal government is especially under an obligation to act when the offense is spread across three states, in the presence of applauding sheriffs and indifferent governors.

EVENING GAZETTE (CEDAR RAPIDS, IA)
April 19, 1921

TO PARDON NEGRO LOUISIANA SHERIFF FORGOT TO HANG.

BATON ROUGE, La., April 19.—The case of Lonnie Eaton, Negro, whom the sheriff of Ouachita Parish "forgot" to hang

February 4, was on the docket for disposal by the State Pardon Board at its meeting here today. Eaton's case caused widespread comment when Sheriff Grant of Ouachita wrote Governor Parker shortly after February 4, that he had been "so rushed with work that he forgot to hang Eaton," who was accused of participation in the murder of a white man.

Attorney General Coco in a written opinion held that Eaton's status was unchanged by the sheriff's oversight, and that there was nothing in the statue books to prevent a future date being set for the execution. Other circumstances taken into consideration, the Attorney General expressed himself in favor of a pardon. His view was seconded by Gov. Parker.

LEBANON (PA) DAILY NEWS
April 21, 1921

MAN SHERIFF FORGOT TO HANG WAS GIVEN LIFE SENTENCE. LONNIE EATON HAD SMILE A YARD WIDE.

(Special to *News* by United Press.)
SHREVEPORT, La., April 21.—Lonnie Eaton, a negro prisoner, wore the "insuppressible smile" here today because he had been sentenced to life imprisonment. Lonnie is the murderer that the sheriff "forgot to hang" on the date of his execution. For weeks, the troublesome question of what to do with Lonnie has been bothering the county officials. Today the State Board of Pardons announced the death penalty had been commuted to life imprisonment.

HAMILTON (OHIO) EVENING JOURNAL
April 25, 1921

EDITORIAL COMMENTS. LONNIE EATON CASE.

Sentiment and justice are strange. Lonnie Eaton committed murder. Without hesitation he was sentenced to hang. Nobody fussed about that. The sheriff was too busy and forgot to hang him on the day fixed. Now he will not hang him at all. Imprisonment for life instead. How would you analyze that? It is a good thing, of course, whenever the public refrains from setting the example to the murderer by capital punishment. What about the "sentiment" involved?

DENTON (TX) RECORD CHRONICLE
October 18, 1921

BOWIE COUNTY MOB COMPOSED LARGELY OF NEGROES SEEKS TO LYNCH ONE OF THEIR OWN RACE.

HOUSTON, Texas, October 18.—Eddie Hopkins, negro, charged with the murder of his wife, today was safe in jail at Texarkana, escaping death at the hands of a mob composed principally of members of his own race.

EVENING INDEPENDENT (MASSILLON, OH)
April 30, 1923

50 WOMEN HELP TO LYNCH MAN.

COLUMBIA, MO., April 30.—James T. Scott, identified by fourteen-year-old Regina Almstedt, daughter of a University of Missouri professor, as the man who tried to attack her was taken from the jail early Sunday morning and hanged.

The mob numbered 500, and among them were about 50 women. They employed an acetylene torch to open the door of the cell after they had worked from shortly before midnight, battering their way past two doors of the jail.

During the half hour that the torch was doing its work cutting away the lock of the prisoner's cell, Scott stood behind the bars protesting his innocence and begging to be allowed a fair trial. Hundreds followed the mob as it marched the man fully three-quarters of a mile to a bridge.

As Scott was about to be thrown from the bridge, he declared his innocence. "Before God, gentlemen," the doomed man spoke, "I am innocent." Raucous shouts of derision were raised as Scott prayed.

1925 Lynching of unnamed African American, location unknown.

EVENING INDEPENDENT (MASSILLON, OH)

April 30, 1923

MOB LEADERS FACE ARREST FOR MURDER.

(By Associated Press)

COLUMBUS, Mo., April 30.—Leaders of the mob which stormed the county jail here Sunday morning, and hanged James Scott, negro, charged with attacking the 14-year-old daughter of Dr. H.F. Almstedt, head of the German Department of the University of Missouri, are known according to R.M. Hulen, county prosecuting attorney, who promises an immediate grand jury investigation. At least one non-resident of Columbia led the mob, it is said. Eyewitnesses denied students were in the mob. The girl was not injured in the alleged attack.

WASHINGTON POST
March 21, 1925

NEGRO IS LYNCHED BY 2,000 VIRGINIANS. MOB AT WAVERLY HANGS HIM TO TREE, RIDDLES CORPSE, AND BURNS IT.

Norfolk, Va., March 20.—A negro, charged with attacking a white woman, was taken from the Sussex County jail at Waverly, Va., early tonight and lynched by a mob estimated at 2,000 persons. The negro, who was known as "Shorty" and said to have recently gone to Waverly from Franklin, was said to have been positively identified by the victim of the attack. As the news of his arrest spread, a crowd surrounded the jail, "covered" Sheriff T. B. Farrin and his deputies with shotguns, and smashed the door of the jail. The prisoner, who in the meantime was said to have confessed, was taken to a vacant lot and strung up to a tree where his body was riddled with shot, and later cut down and burned.

WASHINGTON POST
June 14, 1927

2 BURNED AT STAKE BY MISSISSIPPI MOB

Louisville. Miss., June 13.—(By A. P.).—Two negroes, accused of having slain Clarence Nichols, a sawmill superintendent, were seized by a mob early today, paraded through the streets of Louisville and then taken a short distance from town, where they were tied to a telephone post and burned to death.

W. S Permenter, deputy sheriff, and two other officers were taking the negroes to Jackson for safekeeping. They were overtaken near Noxapater by a mob, which blocked the highway and demanded the prisoners. The officers at first refused to surrender them, and fired several shots into the air in an effort to frighten the mob, whose number was estimated at 1,000, but the mob was insistent.

After gaining possession of the slayers, the crowd brought them back to Louisville and marched through the principal streets. Then as daylight neared they went into the country, tied them to the improvised funeral pyre, poured several cans of gasoline on them, and struck a match.

The negroes' terrified screams apparently touched one member of the mob, who was said to have attempted to extinguish the blaze, but was seized by others and forced back. It was understood neither victim made any statement.

TIME MAGAZINE
Monday, Oct. 10, 1927

RACES: JIM CROW JR.

Youth is brave, but youth is cruel. Last week, two dozen young Negroes of Gary, Ind., were mortified by 1,357 young whites of Gary, Ind., probably more painfully than any adult Negro ever lynched by rabid adult whites.

The thing began when the pupils of Emerson High School returned to their classes and found the 24 Negroes enrolled in their midst. Emerson High School is in the "nice" residential section of Gary. It has never before had more than four or five Negro pupils. But during the summer, Gary's school districts were redefined. Because they lived where they did, the 24 Negroes were entitled by law to attend Emerson High School.

Law or no law, the Emerson pupils whispered, gestured, glowered at the dusky newcomers. They told their parents, who protested to Superintendent William A. Wirt and Principal A. E. Spaulding, who said nothing could be done. "Segregation is impossible because of economic reasons," said Mr. Wirt as tactfully as possible.

Winfield Eschelman of the Emerson senior class, glib talker, good swimmer, got together with Jack Keener, sleek cheerleader, and Sam Chase, smart debater, and some of the athletically "big men" of Emerson, to talk things over. Result: on Monday morning, instead of attending classes, some 800 Emersonians in floppy trousers, sporty sweaters, trim skirts, and fetching blouses, went shouting and laughing through Gary's business section. Police disbanded them for "obstructing traffic" but many of them later stood around outside Emerson High School, hissing, gibing, and catcalling at non-striking students when school let out. Policemen saw to it that the 24 Negroes went home unmolested.

Next day the "nice" residential part of Gary was littered and scrawled with placards and signs:

"WE WON'T GO BACK UNTIL EMERSON IS WHITE. . . . NO NIGGERS FOR EMERSON. . . . EMERSON IS A WHITE MAN'S SCHOOL," etc., etc.

The strikers' ranks swelled to 900 that day. Then, emboldened by their elders' actions or kept at home by nervous parents, Emerson's seventh and eighth grades walked out, making a total of 1,357 strikers. Police broke up attempted Negro mass meetings. The school authorities threatened the strikers in vain.

Led by talkative Winfield Eschelman, the strikers formulated their demands at a mass meeting, which the school officials attended: 1) Let all Negroes be segregated in corners of Emerson classrooms and in the school cafeteria. 2) Let no disciplinary reprisals be made upon the strikers when they should return. 3) Let the strikers not have to "make up" school work missed during the strike. 4) Let the Emerson Negroes be transferred to other schools as soon as possible.

5) Let an all-Negro high school be built in Gary as soon as possible.

The school authorities were helpless. President Ralph Snyder of the Board of Safety, representing Mayor Floyd E. Williams, arbitrated the situation and the strikers won all their demands. Magnanimous, Winfield Eschelman and friends permitted three Negro seniors to finish out the year at Emerson because they had been there all along, but the rest were transferred temporarily to an all-Negro junior high school elsewhere in town. The strikers returned to classes.

The issue then shifted to the City Council, a special sitting of which was called to hurry through a $15,000 temporary all-Negro high school. The galleries were packed with "race people" who came to hear their viewpoint at last expressed without hindrance, by three Negro Councilmen. The Council has 15 members, and in the absence of three white members, the three Negroes were sufficient to block the passage of the $15,000 temporary appropriation, which required a two-thirds council vote.

Negro Alderman A. B. Whitlock did not insinuate that Ku Klux Klannism lay behind the Emerson strike. Instead, he firmly said: "This [appropriation] is a useless expenditure of the taxpayers' money. We have plenty of room now for all the schoolchildren of Gary. This money [$15,000] would not equip a shack, and the site you propose is in a wilderness. There are no streets, no sewers, and no facilities there at all."

White Alderman Merritt Martindale, senior Councilman, interrupted Mr., Whitlock. "Now, Bill." he said, "I hope you're not going to take a wrong view of us whites. The difference is there and it does no good to try to hide it."

"My people are taxpayers," protested Colored Alderman William Burrus. "They have a right to as good an education as anyone. You are setting an awful example by yielding to these striking students. . . . These young people are taking the law into their own hands."

The whites promised that a $60,000 permanent high school would be built for Negroes as soon as possible. A

Negro replied: "Even if you offered us a million-dollar school we wouldn't take it. We're fighting for the principle of the thing"

Numbers won. When the three absent white members were obtained for another council meeting, the two-thirds vote went through. Gary is to have $15,000 temporary quarters for the Emerson High Negroes. More suitable, permanent all-Negro quarters will probably be furnished in time.

Pondering this outcome, students of U. S. race problems reflected that 95% of all U. S. Negroes are descended from slave stock, some of which has been in the U. S. even longer than genuine Mayflower stock. They also reflected that, whereas U. S. Negroes form 14% of Gary's population, U. S. whites form 36%; foreign-born whites form 50%. Thus a large majority of Winfield Eschelman & friends were—if representative of Gary's population—descended 14% from Slavs, 10% from Poles, 4% from Hungarians, 3% from Austrians, 3% from Croats, 3% from Italians, 2% from Germans, 1% from Greeks, 1% from Mexicans, 8% from miscellaneous white races, 1% from races of other colors.

WASHINGTON POST
May 31, 1928

MASKED BAND SEIZES MISSOURI PRISONER.

MARSHALL, Mo., May 30 (A.P.)—Ocie Wilson, a negro, who yesterday shot and killed Romeo Logan; another negro, at Slater, was taken from officers on the highway between here and Slater early today by twelve masked men. The sheriff's office here reported no trace of Wilson had been found early this afternoon, and officers did not know whether Wilson had been taken by friends of Logan bent on lynching him. The officers believe the men were negroes. A report that Wilson's body had been found hanging to a tree south of Slater proved unfounded.

WASHINGTON POST

March 11, 1930

KLANSMAN IS FINED IN CANADIAN RAID.

OAKVILLE, Ontario, March 10 (N.Y. W.N.S.). —Members of the Ku Klux Klan in Canada found today that the time honored phrase, "A man's home is his castle," still holds good in British jurisprudence when C.W.A. Phillips, leader of a band of white-robbed Klansmen who invaded this town last week carrying a fiery cross and took a white girl from the house of her common-law Negro husband. He was fined $50 with an alternative of 30 days in jail in police court.

The case has aroused wide interest as the first in Canada involving the Klan. More than 100 Klansmen were involved in the raid. Defense protested that the Klansmen had acted in orderly fashion, and drew and admission from the girl, Isabella Jones, that she was living with Ira Johnson "immorally."

BALTIMORE NEWS

December 5, 1931

MOB DESCRIBED BY BROCKMAN

Ed Brockman, well-known boxing referee of Baltimore, and two Baltimore boxers, Andy Kelly and Heinie Welch, were in Salisbury to take part in a fight program last night. Brockman today told his story of the lynching of Matthew Williams, part of which he witnessed.

Out of the pocket of his overcoat he pulled a six-inch length of rope, a "souvenir" given to him by a man who claimed it was cut from the rope with which the negro was hanged.

Brockman said:

"We were in the fight club and several hundred persons were waiting for the first bout. I was weighing in Red Shreves and Bud Crosby, who were to fight.

CROWD STAMPEDES

"Suddenly the word came that they were lynching Williams. There was a stampede for the doors. I drove my car a distance of about a mile and a half to the courthouse green and they had just cut the negro down. As I walked around the courthouse, here came the leaders, carrying the body along. As they stepped out into the street they let it drop, and then dragged it by the rope down through the negro part of town.

BOUTS DELAYED.

"Later I saw the fire, but didn't want to go down there. We went back to the fight and the bouts didn't get started until after 10 o'clock. And some of the fighters didn't show up, and only about half the crowd. It was a quiet and orderly mob. I saw no drunks. There were many women."

BALTIMORE AFRO-AMERICAN
December 12, 1931

31 LYNCHINGS IN MARYLAND SINCE THE YEAR 1882. 28 OF THE VICTIMS WERE COLORED, ONLY 3 WERE WHITE.

Since 1882, Maryland has had 31 lynchings, according to Tuskegee Institute Records. Of the victims, 28 were colored and 3 were white.

Records prior to 1882 are not available, but it is known that Maryland slaves, like those in other states, were frequently lynched for the murder of overseers of owners.

The Negro Year Book figures for the U.S. for the decade from 1850 to 1860 alone show 46 slaves put to death for killing overseers or owners of them. 26 of these slaves were lynched.

BALTIMORE AFRO-AMERICAN
December 12, 1931

MOB TOYED WITH BODY FOR 5 HOURS. LYNCHERS IN SALISBURY HAD RIGHT-OF-WAY.

SALISBURY, (Lynch-Town) Md.,—Sober-minded people of the Eastern Shore are hard put in their efforts to fathom the action of Lynch Town's comic opera police, who carried the charred and mutilated body of Matthew Williams out into the woods after the lynching orgy, and covered it with leaves and buried it.

The actions of the police officials were pathetic throughout the whole barbarous demonstration.

When the mob first gathered at the hospital, the authorities were on the scene, but their resistance was so feeble that the victim was dragged from his cot and carried to the scene of the hanging. Here police officials showed another spirit of valor after the youth had been hanged, and after forcing their way through the crowd, demanded the body be cut down.

With the hoots and boos of the milling horde ringing in their ears, the officials were again cowed and made off without retrieving the body from the hoodlums.

Police Went Home.

Whether they went home and went to sleep or not are matters of conjecture, but they did not reappear on the scene until about two hours later when the howling mob was burning the body.

Here they made another feeble effort to rescue the body from the flames, but gruff voices ordered them from the scene of the burning. The brave guardians of the law again skidooed and another hour elapsed. When finally the body had been dragged up and down the street and finally strung up on a lamp post, the ire of the police was finally aroused. With a half dozen of the mob leaders still whooping it up around the burned body the police rushed to the scene and a deputy sheriff is reported to have said: "You boys have been making fools of us long enough. We are going to take that body. You've had your fun now, and you ought to be satisfied."

With everybody too drunk and tired to shoo them off, the body was cut down and the gallant officers had at last performed their duty. Fully five hours had elapsed between the attack on the hospital and recovery of the body by the officials. In the meantime, a unit of state militia was in the city and could have been rounded up in a few minutes. A number of state police could have been called from the sub-stations between Salisbury and

Elkton.

Pull Prize Boner

The Salisbury Police did not reach their heights of comedy until after they had recovered the body. They did not know what to do with it. With the family of the victim clamoring for the remains of their loved one, with a city morgue at their disposal; the police hit upon the original idea of tossing the body into a truck and carrying it several miles out into the country and covering it with burlap and leaves. After they had returned to town and repaired to their respective homes, the officials decided that this was not the proper procedure. They then piled into trucks again, rounded up a colored undertaker, and returned to the spot and brought the body back to the city.

Describes Body.

Eye witnesses to the lynching described the remains of the victim after it had been burned by the mob. The whole upper portion of the body was completely charred beyond recognition. The hair and skin was burned off completely, leaving a skull covered with soot. The eyes were destroyed, leaving only the black holes. The upper portion of the body and the lower limbs were burned to a crisp. With this hideous form the mob leaders toyed and made sport like a cat with a mouse for about five hours.

BALTIMORE AFRO-AMERICAN

December 12, 1931

EYEWITNESS TO LYNCHING TELLS HOW MOB ACTED.

SALISBURY, (Lynch-town) Md.—A detailed account of the lynching of Matthew Williams here Friday night, by an eyewitness, Howard A. Nelson, of South Philadelphia, as told to AFRO-AMERICAN reporters, Sunday. Mr. Nelson is fair of skin and may be colored or white as he pleases.

"I arrived at Salisbury Thursday afternoon on a business trip. Early Friday I went to Princess Anne and returned late in the afternoon. I was standing talking to an acquaintance on Main Street about the killing of that man Elliot, when I noticed a group of men milling about the front of the town paper, the *Salisbury Times*. When I had finished my conversation, I went over to read the bulletin.

"I read the bulletin that was posted on the front of the building. It read:

'Nigger is Dead.
The nigger who murder Mr. Elliot, a prominent citizen, has been reported as being dead.'

"While I was reading this, a white man who was standing by mistook me for one of them and said, 'Ain't that a damn shame that nigger died so soon. There was going to be some fun here tonight.' Just about that time another bulletin was posted. It read: 'The statement made by officials that the Negro was dead is false. A message just received say that he is improving.'

Almost a Command.

"The men stood there for about five minutes. They stood talking in groups; more persons read that bulletin, and the crowd grew ever so thick. Almost like an explosion, someone yelled, 'Let's go to the hospital and get this nigger and lynch him.'

"Almost as though it was a military command, the crowd started toward the hospital. I followed along to see what was going to happen.

"The white man who was walking along side of me said: 'It's going to be good to see that nigger swing.

Curse and Swear.

"When we arrived at the hospital, there was some man who asked the mob not to bother Williams. The crowd started to curse and swear and then a man said to be Dr. Dix came outside and asked the men to be quiet as there were many dangerously ill persons in the hospital. By that time, a group of men—just how many I don't know—had gotten in the hospital and seized Williams. The colored ward is on the first floor towards the rear of the building.

Thrown out Window.

"Instead of carrying the body through the door, the men

threw him out of the first floor window to a large group of men. Williams had on the regulation hospital gown and his head was swathed in bandages which covered his eyes and his feet were bare.

"Seemingly, in a semi-conscious condition, the fellow was dragged to the court house lawn. Someone produced a long rope. After three attempts, they were able to get the rope over a tree right on the Main Street side of the court house, after a small boy was lifted up by men.

Let Him Fall.

"The men who had been holding Williams let him fall to the ground while they helped to get the rope fixed properly. While he was lying on the ground, evidently unconscious, as he did not move, the rope was placed around his neck.

Jerked Up and Down.

"From a prone position, the body was pulled about fifteen feet in the air near to the limb of the tree over which the rope had been placed. The body would be allowed to drop to within two feet of the ground and then suddenly be jerked back. This was done three times. The leader each time would say, 'Pull him up, boys,' and then 'Give him the works, boys.'

Fireman Enter "Show."

"At this point, the fire department apparatus was called out. By whom I do not know, I do not know whether they were ordered to turn the hose on the mob to disperse them or not, but the members of the fire department joined the mob and watched the lynching. They seemed as happy over the lynching as the mobsters.

"The body was left hanging in the air for twenty minutes. The rope had been made fast to the trunk of another tree. While the body was swinging there, the mob yelled. On mention of the names of the mayor sheriff, and the chief of police, the mob booed, but cheered the men who led the mob.

"The were about 2,600 persons in the mob. I had been near the rear and eased my way to the very edge of the mob, which had surrounded the court house grounds and had filled back to the street.

Burn Body.

"The rope was cut and the body fell to the ground with a thud. A couple of men grabbed the part of the rope which still was around the victim's neck and started down Main Street. They went three blocks to a lot bordering the colored residential section.

"Here they forced the attendant of a garage and a filling station to give them gasoline. He refused, and several men of the mob obtained five gallon cans and took 45 gallons of gasoline. They spread newspapers over the body, and then poured on the gasoline. They ignited the paper and as the flames leaped into the air, they sent up a roar which was deafening. The leaders of the mob continued to add the gasoline to the body.

"The stench of the burning flesh was unbearable, and I left, for fear of detection. Just as I started away, the leader of the mob hailed a passing truck and started down Main Street with the mob following. As the truck passed the *Salisbury Times*, a man in the office called to one of the mob leaders and yelled, 'Atta a boy, Jim.'

Tie Body Up.

"At Lake and Main Streets, they tied the burned and charred body to an arc lamp post in front of Rosen's store. The owner of the store is called the chief of police, and had the body cut down after the mob had dispersed.

"While en route to Lake Street, the mob spied two colored men, John Allison and Harold Fisher. They yelled, 'Get those niggers.' When a few of the mob started after the men, Allison jumped over the bridge into the Wicomico River and swam a quarter of a mile and went ashore. Fisher ran into a side street and disappeared.

"City officials had a truck and removed the body to the outskirts of the city, where they left it.

"The police and city officials, with others, can identify the leaders of that mob. At the hospital, the doctors, nurses and police addressed them by name. Every leader in the mob can be identified. I can identify the leader."

Philadelphia Woman Mourns Brother who was Lynched

MRS. OLIVIA SIMMONS
only sister of Matthew Williams, Eastern Shore mob victim, who says yet that she does not believe her brother shot the lumber dealer.

BALTIMORE AFRO-AMERICAN
December 12, 1931

LYNCHED MAN'S SISTER DOESN'T BELIEVE BROTHER A KILLER.

(An exclusive interview with Mrs. Olivia Simmons, sister of the lynched youth, 7118 Gray's Avenue, West Philadelphia.)

SALISBURY, Md.—"For the past six years since my marriage I have been living in Philadelphia. Matt has been referred to by some persons here as being mentally unbalanced. That is not true. He was of good mind and seldom associated with the others who lived in this neighborhood.

"He was fond of motion pictures, baseball and church. He had no bad habits. A Cambridge paper referred to him as being a rowdy and a gun-totter. Never in my life have I known him to have even a small pen knife to carry around. He used a small knife at the box factory which he never brought away. He was never arrester or reprimanded by an officer.

"I don't believe that Matt shot Mr. Elliot," the young woman declared emphatically. "He had been working at the factory for nine years. He was considered a good worker by the members of the Elliot family and oftentimes trusted with valuables that the others would not be trusted with. He went to the Elliot home whenever he desired and was treated very kindly.

"He admired Mr. Elliot, his son, and both of their wives. I can't see how it was that Matt shot Mr. Elliot. In my heart I shall never believe it."

Questioned as to her belief, Mrs. Simmons answered, stating "There is something about it that I am at a loss to explain; still I can't believe what they say that Matt did."

Maryland, My Maryland!
THE BALTIMORE SUN
DEC 6 1931

NEW YORK TIMES
October 19, 1933

BOY SLASHES NEGRO'S EAR.

[By The Associated Press]

PRINCESS ANNE, MARYLAND, Oct. 18.—The march to the scene of the lynching of Armwood was wild in the extreme. The mob members seemed crazed, continually leaping on the Negro, even after he fell to the ground, and was unable to rise. One boy, apparently about 18 years old, slashed the Negro's ear almost off with a knife. Under the oak tree, despite the presence of women and children, all the victim's clothes were torn from his body, and he hung there for some minutes nude.

After they had burned the body, the mob members disbanded. In the meantime, John Richardson, a white man who was under arrest, charged with being an accessory after the fact in the assault on the farm woman, was taken from the jail by officers, and was started for Baltimore. He was accused of taking the Negro away from the vicinity of the alleged attack, and transporting him to another section of the county. Threats made by the mob members caused officers to take this precaution.

CHRISTIAN SCIENCE MONITOR
October 19, 1933

NEGRO LYNCHED.

PRINCESS ANNE, Md., Oct. 19.—(AP),.—Gov. Albert C. Ritchie has directed Judge Robert F. Duer and Mr. John B. Robins, State's Attorney, to take the necessary legal steps to bring to justice those guilty of lynching George Armwood, Negro, charged with attacking an 81-year-old woman. Armwood was seized from 25 state policemen at the jail here last night by a mob of more than 1,000 persons, and hanged. It was the first lynching in Maryland since 1931.

NEW YORK TIMES
October 21, 1933

URGES RITCHIE ACT IN NEGRO'S LYNCHING

[Special to THE NEW YORK TIMES]

BALTIMORE, Oct. 20. — Dr. Broadus Mitchell of Johns Hopkins University demanded at a Governor's hearing today that Governor Ritchie take steps looking to impeachment of Judge Robert F. Duer as a result of the lynching Wednesday night of George Armwood, Negro. The hearing was accorded to several societies after pleas had been made to the Governor for a thorough investigation of the lynching of Armwood, who was accused of attacking a white woman.

Representatives of the National Association for the Advancement of Colored People, the Socialist party, the National Urban League, the Labor Defense League, the Colored Ministerial Union, Republican and Democratic colored organizations were present. Governor Ritchie said that an investigation of the lynching would be made by Attorney General W. Preston Lane and others.

"Failure" by Maryland authorities to accord to Negroes their rights under the Constitution may result in an appeal to Attorney General Cummings, Bernard Ades, attorney for the Labor Defense League, said tonight.

DANVILLE (VA) BEE
November 29, 1933

EYE-WITNESS ACCOUNT OF MO. LYNCHING.

ST. JOSEPH, Mo., Nov. 29.—(AP)—The following eye-witness account of the lynching of Lloyd Warner, 19-year-old negro, was given by A.M. (Pat) Olmsted, local politician.

After reaching the third floor of the jail building, the leaders of the mob were met by Sheriff Otto Thiesen, who unlocked the cell where Warner was cowering.

"Stripped to the waist, the prisoner was dragged out by four young members of the mob.

"As the four carried him struggling down the stairs other members of the mob followed, kicking, and beating the prisoner. They cheered, shouted, and cursed.

"He was taken through the north grill door of the jail, which had been wrecked by means of a huge truck.

"Once outside the building, the mob hesitated, undecided whether to take Warner to the scene of the crime, about 18 blocks east of the jail.

"Reaching the tree, a rope was brought up and placed about the victim's neck. He attempted to talk, but shouts of "string him up," drowned out his pleas.

"He was raised about 8 feet off the ground. The crowd let out a big cheer.

"It was over in a fcw minutes.

"A group of men then rushed to an oil station across the street and obtained some gasoline with which they soaked the body. Torches were applied.

"Later a big fire was built under the body.

"This burned the rope in two, and the body fell to the ground. Souvenir hunters rushed forward and began cutting off pieces of the negro's clothing.

"One man fainted and an ambulance was called to revive him."

PORT ARTHUR (TX) NEWS
December 8, 1933

5,000 VICTIMS IN 50 YEARS, GHASTLY LYNCHING RECORD.

FIVE THOUSAND victims in a half-century—that is the black record of lynching in the United States. Even this is a record from which pages are missing, one on which hundreds of names of those who have gone to their graves by violence are not listed, one which does not include those slain in race riots and other outbreaks.

Moreover, before the time, which this record covers, before it was thought worthwhile to investigate lynching, hundreds of others died at the hands of maddened crowds. Crowds, which acted first, and looked into the facts after the grim deed was done.

HUGE INDEMNITY PAID

Twice this happened in the case of Chinese lynched in Wyoming and California, and twice in cases of Italians lynched in California and Louisiana. The indemnity in all these cases totaled more than a $250,000.

The greatest number of persons done to death by mobs in a single year was 235 in 1892. From year to year since, there has been a steady decline in the toll.

But the time is not here for congratulation. In 1932 there were 10 lynchings in the United States. When a mob in San Jose, California dragged two kidnap-slayers from jail and hanged them in a public park. Furthermore, an enraged throng seized a negro in jail at St. Joseph, Mo., and hanged and burned him. The total to date in 1933 amounted to 27, the highest mark since 1926, when there were 38 lynchings.

OAKLAND (CA) TRIBUNE
November 27, 1933

CROWD "CELEBRATES" AFTER LYNCHING IN SAN JOSE STREETS.

SAN JOSE, Nov. 27.—A spirit of revelry, rivaled only by the observance of a New Year's Eve or Armistice Day, prevailed here last night as San Jose "celebrated" the lynching of Thomas H. Thurmond and John M. Holmes.

After the "park affair" crowds of men, women, and children flocked along the sidewalks of First Street the city's main thoroughfare. Streetcars were blocked at several intersections, and on street corners those who bet that Thurmond and Holmes would not be lynched paid their debts. Shouting and singing could be heard from passing automobiles—with the hangings the sole topic.

A spirit of satisfaction over the mob violence and lynchings prevailed. Throughout the entire procedure, only on dissenting voice was raised. That was when an unidentified man protested the hanging of Thurmond and attempted to cut him down after he had been hanged in St. James Park. He was subdued by leaders of the mob.

Impelled by morbid curiosity, hundreds of persons clung around the two gruesome objects, which dangled from trees in the moonlight of St. James Park last night. White uniformed milkmen, on their morning round, halted near the hanging corpses and the dawn painted the bodies in a ghastly light. Streetcar conductors and motormen, telephone operators, and others whose work kept them out during the night, paused briefly to view the work of the lynchers, peered inside the battered door of Santa Clara County Jail, and then went on their way.

OAKLAND (CA) TRIBUNE
November 27, 1933

MEN AND WOMEN BATTLE FOR LYNCHED MAN'S CLOTHING.

SAN JOSE, Nov. 27.—Thousands of men and women battled hand to hand last night for scraps of cloth from the trousers of Thomas Thurmond, hanged by an infuriated mob for the kidnapping and murder of Brook E. Hart. They were the souvenir hunters. When they had dispersed by police, they had virtually stripped the trees from which Thurmond and his accomplice, John M. Holmes (white), were executed. The county jail was in shambles.

As the body of Thurmond hung, with the feet seven feet from the ground, men and women closed in upon it and tore the trousers away. A battle royal followed, in which women and men were trampled. Knives appeared in the melee, and the prized bit of clothing was torn into shreds, the winners carrying away their hard-won trophies.

SHIRT BURNED OFF.

As the fight was in progress, an unidentified member of the mob struck a match and applied it to the lower part of Thurmond's shirt. A moment later his shirt, vest, and coat were in flames. They were extinguished when his body was cut down, but his body was badly seared. Meanwhile, a mad scramble was in progress in from of the county jail, across the street from St. James Park, where the execution took place.

Prizes there were the shells of tear gas bombs, resembling hand grenades, thrown into the crowd by deputy sheriffs earlier in a vain attempt to prevent the abduction of Thurmond and Holmes. One enterprising souvenir hunter climber into the elm tree from which Thurmond was hanged and sawed off the entire limb, measuring about five inches in diameter, from which the body hung.

LIMB SAWED OFF.

After the limb fell, there was a mad battle for twigs and bark. At the same time, other souvenir collectors were plying knives on the trunks of the two trees. Bits of rope used in the double lynching were highly prized mementos. At least three prizes went undisturbed, presumably because of their size and weight, they were the three pipes used to batter in the steel door to the jail. They were 15 feet long and 5 inches in diameter. Two lay in the corridor of the jail and one lay near the tree where Holmes was hanged.

Windows were broken out of the county jail; furniture was shattered, first to be used as clubs, second to be carried away as souvenirs. In addition, the lighting facilities were put out of commission. The body of Holmes was not molested by the mob as it hung from the limb of a second elm tree, for it was nude. It was viewed however, by thousands of men, women, and children.

OAKLAND (CA) TRIBUNE

November 27, 1933

MORGUE UNITES KILLERS AND THEIR VICTIM.

SAN JOSE, Nov. 27.—In the same morgue today lie the bodies of Brooke Hart, wealthy San Jose youth, and of John M. Holmes and Thomas Harold Thurmond, who paid for his kidnapping and murder by the swift justice of "lynch law." Members of Holmes' family are planning for his funeral, but today none of Thurmond' relatives had even gone to view his body.

Hart's body was taken to the morgue yesterday shortly after its recovery. Twelve hours later the corpses of
Thurmond and Holmes were cut down from trees in St. James

Park by deputy coroners and placed on slabs in rooms adjoining those in which Hart's remains lay.

Coroner Amos Williams stated that Maurice Holmes, father of John, went to the morgue shortly after the lynching and identified the body of his son. His comments, Williams declared, were brief and matter-of-fact. "He appeared to have his emotion under iron control." Williams commented. Holmes gave no instructions for the disposal of the body. His wife, however, said that she and her husband are waiting to confer with other members of the family before going ahead with funeral plans.

MOB SEEKS SOUVENIRS.

"Throw them in the bay!" "Feed em to the crabs!" were the shouts that greeted officers who removed the bodies. The deputies were offered no real resistance except by souvenir hunters who rushed in attempting to obtain the rope or bits of clothing as the officials climbed the tree and cut down the bodies. The officers removed the bodies so quickly, that they did not even remove the ropes form the victims' necks.

After the body of Holmes was removed, one member of the crowd climbed the tree and sawed off the limb from which Holmes hanged. He offered it for sale at "50 cents an inch."

LYNCHED — George Armwood just before he was hanged and burned at Princess Anne, Md. The N.A.A.C.P. seeks the passage of a bill to punish lynchers.

George Armwood, image source: privately owned NAACP flyer.

George Armwood image source: privately owned NAACP flyer

WASHINGTON POST
November 29, 1933

LYNCH VICTIM'S BODY DUG UP CROWD OF 150 MEN OPENS GRAVE OF ARMWOOD AT POOR FARM.

PRINCESS ANNE, Md., Nov. 28 (Special).—The body of George

Armwood, Negro, lynched by a mob here October 18, was removed from its grave at the county poor farm tonight. Steve Hopkins, superintendent of the poor farm, told of the body being removed. He said the coffin was left beside the open grave.

At about 9 o'clock, automobiles began arriving at the poor farm. By 9:30, about 50 cars had gathered and 150 min had grouped around the grave. Two of the men with spades began digging, and the coffin was lifted to the surface and opened. Their purpose apparently accomplished, the men quietly returned to their automobiles and drove away.

DANVILLE (VA) BEE

November 29, 1933

EYEWITNESS ACCOUNT OF MO. LYNCHING.

ST JOSEPH, MO., Nov. 29.—(AP)—The following eye-witness account of the lynching of Lloyd Warner, 19-year-old negro, was given by A.M. (Pat) Olmstead, a local politician.

After reaching the third floor of the jail building, the leaders of the mob were met by Sheriff Otto Thiegen, who unlocked the cell where Warner was cowering.

"Stripped to the waist, the prisoner was dragged out by four young members of the mob.

"As the four carried him struggling down the stairs other members of the mob followed, kicking, and beating the prisoner. They cheered, shouted and cursed.

"He was taken through the north grill door of the jail, which had been wrecked by means of a huge truck.

"Once outside the building, the mob hesitated, undecided whether to take Warner to the scene of the crime, about 18 blocks east of the jail.

Some in the crowd, however, expressed impatience and, at the suggestion of someone he was rushed about a block away to a huge elm tree across from the courthouse lawn.

"Reaching the tree a rope was brought up and placed about the victim's neck. He attempted to talk, but shouts of "string him up," drowned out his pleas.

"He was raised about eight feet off the ground. The crowd let out a bug cheer.

"It was over in a few minutes.

"A group of men then rushed to an oil station across the street and obtained some gasoline with which, they soaked the body. Torches were applied.

"Later, a big fire was built under the body."

"This burned the rope in two, and the body fell to the ground. Souvenir hunters rushed forward and began cutting of pieces of the negro's clothing.

"One man fainted and an ambulance was called to revive him."

BIG SPRINGS (TX) HERALD
December 22, 1933

KILLERS ACT QUIETLY.

COLUMBIA, Tenn., (AP) Riddled with bullets first, a young negro which a grand jury refused to indict on a charge of an attempted attack on an orphan girl, 11, was lynched here early Saturday.

The body was found suspended from a rope tied to the limb of a tree, after Sheriff Godwin received an anonymous telephone call advising he would find "a dead negro at the forks of the road," nearby.

The mob acted quietly and without the knowledge of officers. The negro, Cord Cheek had been kept in Nashville for safekeeping after a grand jury returned a no-bill on the charge. Officers were unable to find anyone connected with the lynching.

TIME MAGAZINE
November 5, 1934

RACES: THEY DONE ME WRONG

Life in Greenwood, Fla. was a little less dull one day last week when all the white folks in the neighborhood were invited out to George Cannidy's place for a lynching. Someone had dragged Farmer Cannidy's young daughter Lola out across his cotton patch, raped her near a pigsty, bashed in her head, and left her under some pine boughs for dead. A Negro buck named Claude Neal had been arrested for the crime, lodged for safekeeping in a jail across the Alabama line at Brewton. One hundred Floridians had driven over to Brewton and without much fuss removed Claude Neal from the jail.

Upon invitation of a "lynching committee" of six, 5,000 men, women, and children choked the front yard of the Cannidy place, overflowed into the cotton field where bonfires were lighted. The Cannidys had prepared some sharp sticks and whetted their knives in anticipation of the revenge they would take on Negro Neal. A man said to be a Florida legislator got up and amused the crowd with a funny speech as it waited for the spectacle. It was nearly midnight when one of the "lynching committee" appeared to announce that he feared violence with so many people around; there would be no show until most of the mob went home.

Plain truth seemed to be that the lynching committee had so brutalized the Negro that he had died back in the woods on the banks of the Chipola River before the lynchers had a chance to kill him publicly. He was certainly quite dead when, toward morning, the lynchers dumped his mutilated corpse in front of the Cannidy's door. "Pa" Cannidy was hopping mad.

"They done me wrong about this here killing," he wailed. "They promised me they'd bring him up to my house before they killed him and let me have the first shot. That's what I wanted." "Pa" and "Ma" and the eight Cannidy children had to be satisfied with the last shot. They got out the family rabbit gun and pumped a few slugs into the lifeless black moor.

Then the corpse was taken into Marianna, the county seat, and hung up in front of the courthouse. The dirty work of cutting it down went to the county sheriff. National Guardsmen arrived, as usual, too late to do Claude Neal any good. Governor David Holtz, back at Tallahassee from the American Legion convention in Miami (see above), felt that an explanation was due with regard to his tardiness in calling out the militia. "It was not a case of calling out the militia to protect the jail or a prisoner in custody of an officer," said he. "The Negro was held in the hands of a mob out in the woods. It would have been futile to have called out the militia."

But the Association of Southern Women for the Prevention of Lynching, which had begged for troops as soon as Neal was taken from Brewton, found it hard to believe that soldiers were trained only to find their way around in city streets or jail corridors. Indignantly A. S. W. P. L. wired Attorney General Cummings to beg him to start some sort of Federal prosecution.

Harry Sternberg, *Southern Holiday,* 1935, lithograph, 21 x 15 inches. Courtesy of Susan Teller Gallery.

Personal Letter from Eleanor Roosevelt to Walter White detailing the First Lady's lobbying efforts for federal action against lynchings, (National Association for the Advancement of Colored People Records), March 19, 1936.

My dear Mr. White:

Before I received your letter today I had been in to the President, talking to him about your letter enclosing that of the Attorney General. I told him that it seemed rather terrible that one could get nothing done and that I did not blame you for this very serious question. I asked him if there were any possibility of getting even one step taken, and he said the difficulty is that it is unconstitutional apparently for the Federal Government to step in in the lynching situation. The Government has only been allowed to do anything about kidnapping because of its interstate aspect, and even that has not yet been appealed so they are not sure that it will be declared constitutional.

The President feels that lynching is a question of education in the states, rallying good citizens, and creating public opinion so that the localities themselves will wipe it out. However, if it were done by a Northerner, it will have an antagonistic effect. I will talk to him again about the Van Nuys resolution and will try to talk to Senator Byrnes and get his point of view. I am deeply troubled by the whole situation as it seems to be a terrible thing to stand by and let it continue and feel that one cannot speak out as to his feeling. I think your next step would be to talk to the more prominent members of the Senate.

Very sincerely yours,
Eleanor Roosevelt

[5]

TITONKA (IOWA) TOPIC
March 14, 1940

"THE NAME IS FAMILIAR"—LYNCH LAW.

LYNCHING is another well-known American word that is spelled with a small letter but was derived, nevertheless, from the name of a person. Everyone regards lynching merely as the hanging of a suspected criminal by a vengeful mob—but, no one ever gives any thought to the fact that we had no such word to express that idea until Charles Lynch began, with popular support, to take the law into his own hands—or at least, into his own living room—during the Revolution.

Charles Lynch was born in Lynchburg, Va., in 1736. During the Revolutionary war, Tories plundered the countryside and there was a plot in the community to overthrow the Continental government. Mr. Lynch, with some of his neighbors, decided to

[5] Picture of, "The Old Lynch House."*Titonka (Iowa) Topic*, March 14, 1940.

punish this form of lawlessness and, under Lynch's direction, suspected persons were brought to his house and tried. Those convicted were sentenced to receive 39 lashes and were hanged from a walnut tree (shown in the picture above) by their thumbs until they shouted "Liberty forever."

"Lynch law" and "lynching" became terms used to express the situation when citizens take the law into their own hands. But Charles Lynch never "lynched" anyone in the modern sense of the word because he never imposed the death penalty.

WASHINGTON POST
July 5, 1940

WHAT IS A LYNCHING?

A spirited controversy arose last May when Mrs. Jessie Daniel Ames of the Association of Southern Woman for the Prevention of Lynching issued a statement claiming that 12 consecutive months had passed without a lynching in the United States. Her assertion was immediately challenged by a number of correspondents whose letters were published in *The Post.*

Probably the most specific contradiction of this claim came from Mr. Walter White, secretary of the Nation Association for the Advancement of Colored People. In our letter column of May 21st, Mr. White declared that the "Fulton County Grand Jury and the Federal Bureau of Investigation have turned up three mob murders by the Ku Klux Klan almost under the window of Ames' office in Atlanta, Ga." Those "lynchings" were said to have taken place last March. Another chapter in the controversy is now written by President Patterson of Tuskegee Institute. Under date of June 30, he writes:

"According to the information compiled in the department records and research, there is no record of a lynching for the first six months of 1940. This information is based on news releases and on investigations made by persons living in various areas.

So we are confronted by the question: what is a lynching? Were the cases in Georgia lynchings or gang slayings? If "lynching," means taking a prisoner of the hands of law enforcement officers and putting him to death, then the Georgia slayings seem to be outside that classification. If it means any slaying by a mob or gang, then lynching has not yet disappeared.

In at least one respect, this controversy should have a salutary effect. It seems to have put some advocates of the anti-lynching bill on record in favor of Federal action against gangs that resort to murder. There are various types of gang or mob murder, including those for which Chicago and New York have been notorious. Certainly, there would be no point in passing a law designed to counteract one particularly barbaric type of slaying, which seems to be extinct, while ignoring the more prevalent forms of murder, which are still a grave problem.

This controversy has helped to emphasize that murder is a ghastly crime whether it is perpetrated by an infuriated mob, by fanatical vigilantes, professional gangsters, or amateur bandits. It is indisputable that more effective methods of eliminating murders of every type are needed.

The public welfare would be served if all the groups that have interested themselves in the unconstitutional anti-lynching bill would drop that politics-ridden measure, and work for more effective means of protecting human life within the framework of our Federal system.

MIDDLESBORO (KY) DAILY NEWS
July 8, 1949

ARRAIGN THREE FOR FATAL BEATING OF NEGRO TENANT.

HOUSTON, Miss., July 8.—Three white men were to be arraigned on murder charges here today for the fatal beating of a Negro tenant farmer whom they said "hogged the road" with his wagon. Deputy Sheriff T.A. Bryant identified the men as:
James Moore of Thorne, Miss.; Eunice Gore, a soldier stationed at Kessler Field, Miss.; and James (Red) Keelum, also of Thorne. All were said to be in their early 20's.

The victim was Malcolm Wright, 15, Negro. The scene of the attack was on the Thorne road about 11/2 miles northwest of Houston. Bryant said Wright was beat on to death with an automobile jack handle right before his wife and four children about 3 p.m. last Saturday.

Bryant said that feeling in the area was "pretty hot" against the white men, because Wright was a hard working, respected man.

DELTA DEMOCRAT TIMES (GREENSVILLE, MS)

Februarys 16, 1950

TUSKEGEE DEFINES LYNCHING MEANING

TUSKEGEE, Ala., (UP)—Dr. F.D. Patterson, Tuskegee president, today defined the ruling upon which the institute bases its decision on whether a violent death is listed as a lynching.

His explanation came in connection with Washington protests by Rep. Thomas G. Abernethy, D., Miss., on the listing of a Mississippi lynching.

Patterson said, "Tuskegee classes as a lynching, any violent death in which three or more persons take the law into their own hands, and deprive another of his rights without due process."

The Mississippi congressman had written to the institute asking that it delete from the lynch classification the death of Malcolm Wright, in Chickasaw County, Miss., last year. Abernethy contended that it might have been murder or manslaughter, but was "definitely not a lynching."

NORTH ADAMS (MA) TRANSCRIPT

March 19, 1955

A USEFUL WORD—BUT HAVE YOU EVER JOINED A MOB?

A MOB according to my dictionary is a "disorderly assemblage of people." But Mr. Webster has a hard time with the word and makes several tries at it. If you read all the definitions you get the impression that a mob must be composed of people in the lower classes of society—"the masses." The dictionary most surprisingly adds that it is "a disparaging word, except in Australia."

Does this mean that in Australia mobs are made up of nine people? And, as for mobs anywhere in the world, I think Mr. Webster has started out on the wrong foot. This gives me a great deal of satisfaction because I have a good friend who is one of the dictionary's senior editors, and I am always eager to catch him off base.

A MOB in my opinion can be composed of ladies and gentlemen in "high sassiety," of toughs and rough necks, or of any and all sorts of people mixed up together. A mob is any large assemblage of people who have stopped thinking as individuals and are governed by a single arousing emotion, such as anger or greed, or fear, or blinding enthusiasm, or desires for vengeance. "Mob" is an understandable word when it means just that, and a useful one.

I have seen a mob of shoppers jamming the doors of a shop, which has an unusual sale. They are stepping on one another feet and tearing one another's clothes, and maybe one faints, and gets badly mauled; and later we may learn that quite a number of highly respectable ladies were mixed up in it, though they hate to admit it.

Many times in the past there have been religious exhorters loose in the land who have been able to turn congregations into frenzied mobs, and made hundreds of "converts" whose conversion lasted for only a day or an hour. In other words there can be religious mobs, patriotic mobs, witch-hunting mobs, and frightened mobs.

But I wish the meaning of that word could be stretched a little further to include groups of people who might not be together bodily in one place, but they all have caught the same emotional contagion wherever they are, and cannot think for themselves anymore, but only run amok.

A wave of ignorant fear can make a mob. There has been a panic in more than one coastal resort over news of sea serpents. I recall hearing of a village, which became panic-stricken over rumors of a strange wild beast prowling at night. Children were kept close at home; and a group of bold hunters finally made an organized mob. They found a spoiled calf search for his mother. Were you once a little nervous about flying saucers?

NEW YORK TIMES
May 27, 1961

ATTORNEY GENERAL FORESEES A NEGRO U.S. PRESIDENT.

WASHINGTON, May 26.—Attorney General Robert F. Kennedy, in a broadcast to the world over the Voice of America, today acknowledged that the United States flaws in the areas of equal rights for Negroes. He said, however, that steps forward were being made in that area so quickly that, "There's no question that in the next thirty to forty years a Negro can achieve the position . . . of President of the United States."

WASHINGTON POST, TIMES HERALD
November 16, 1965

NEGRO GRAVE DUG UP IN ARMS CACHE HUNT.

GREENVILLE, Miss., Nov. 15 (UPI)—County law officers dug up a Negro's grave today at the urging of white men wearing Ku Klux Klan emblems, but failed to find a promised cache of arms." It's only a poor man's grave," said Greenville police Chief W. C. Burnley.

The digging was done in the early morning under lights, as 13 cars of armed policemen protected the area. A group of white men from out of town, driving a radio-equipped car with Mississippi license tags, had told Burnley that a large "cache of arms for the Black Muslims" had been hidden in the grave. They refused to identify themselves, but wore neckties initialed with a rosette and iron cross, a Klan emblem." I have heard this sort of rot a hundred times," Chief Burnley said later. "They're always giving us tips that are just as crazy as they are."

LOOK MAGAZINE
January 24, 1956, Pgs. 46–50.

THE SHOCKING STORY OF APPROVED KILLING IN MISSISSIPPI.

EDITOR'S NOTE: In the long history of man's inhumanity to man, racial conflict has produced some of the most horrible examples of brutality. The recent slaying of Emmett Till in Mississippi is a case in point. The editors of LOOK are convinced that they are presenting here, for the first time, the real story of that killing – the story no jury heard and no newspaper reader saw. By WILLIAM BRADFORD HUIE-published and disclosed here is the true account of the slaying in Mississippi of a Negro youth named Emmett Till. Last September in Sumner, Miss., a petit jury found the youth's admitted abductors not guilty of murder. In November, in Greenwood, a grand jury declined to indict them for kidnapping.

Of the murder trial, the *Memphis Commercial Appea*l said: "Evidence necessary for convicting on a murder charge was lacking." But with truth absent, hypocrisy and myth have flourished. Now, hypocrisy can be exposed; myth dispelled. Here are the facts. Carolyn Holloway Bryant is 21, five feet tall, weighs 103 pounds. An Irish girl, with black hair and black eyes, she is a small farmer's daughter who, at 17, quit high school at Indianola, Miss., to marry a soldier, Roy Bryant, then 20, now 24. The couple have two boys, three and two; and they operate a store at a dusty crossroads called Money: post office, filling station and three stores clustered around a school and a gin, and set in the vast, lonely cotton patch that is the Mississippi Delta.

Carolyn and Roy Bryant are poor: no car, no TV. They live in the back of the store which Roy's brothers helped set up when he got out of the 82nd Airborne in 1953. They sell "snuff-and-fatback" to Negro field hands on credit: and they earn little because, for one reason, the government has been giving the Negroes food they formerly bought. Carolyn and Roy Bryant's social life is visits to their families, to the Baptist church and, whenever they can borrow a car, to a drive-in, with the kids sleeping in the back seat. They call Shane the best picture they ever saw. For extra money, Carolyn tends store when Roy works outside -- like truck driving for a brother. And he has many brothers. His mother had two husbands, 11 children. The first five -- all boys -- were

"Milam children"; the next six -- three boys, three girls -- were "Bryant children."

This is a lusty and devoted clan. They work, fight, vote and play as a family. The "half" in their fraternity is forgotten. For years, they have operated a chain of cotton field stores, as well as trucks and mechanical cotton pickers. In relation to the Negroes, they are somewhat like white traders in portions of Africa today; and they are determined to resist the revolt of colored men against white rule.

On Wednesday evening, August 24, 1955, Roy was in Texas, on a brother's truck. He had carted shrimp from New Orleans to San Antonio, and proceeded to Brownsville. Carolyn was alone in the store. But back in the living quarters was her sister-in-law Juanita Milam, 27, with her two small sons and Carolyn's two. The store was kept open till 9 on weeknights, 11 on Saturday. When her husband was away, Carolyn Bryant never slept in the store, never stayed there alone after dark. Moreover, in the Delta, no white woman or group of white women ever travels country roads after dark unattended by a man. This meant that during Roy's absences -- particularly since he had no car -- there was family inconvenience. Each afternoon, a sister-in-law arrived to stay with Carolyn until closing time.

Then, the two women, with their children, waited for a brother-in-law to convoy them to his home. Next morning, the sister-in-law drove Carolyn back. Juanita Milam had driven from her home in Glendora. She had parked in front of the store to the left; and under the front seat of this car was Roy Bryant's pistol, a .38 Colt automatic. Carolyn knew it was there. After 9, Juanita's husband, J. W. Milam, would arrive in his pickup to shepherd them to his home for the night.

About 7:30 p.m., eight young Negroes -- seven boys and a girl -- in a '46 Ford had stopped outside. They included sons, grandsons and a nephew of Moses (Preacher) Wright, 64, a 'cropper. They were between 13 and 19 years old. Four were natives of the Delta, and others, including the nephew,

Emmett (Bobo) Till, were visiting from the Chicago area.

Bobo Till was 14 years old: born on July 25, 1941. He was stocky, muscular, weighing about 160, five feet four or five. Preacher later testified: "He looked like a man."

Bobo's party joined a dozen other young Negroes, including

two other girls, in front of the store. Bryant had built checkerboards there. Some were playing checkers, others were wrestling and "kiddin' about girls." Bobo bragged about his white girl. He showed the boys a picture of a white girl in his wallet; and to their jeers of disbelief, he boasted of his success with her.

"You talkin' mighty big, Bo," one youth said. "There's a pretty little white woman in the store. Since you know how to handle white girls, let's see you go in and get a date with her?" "You ain't chicken, are yuh, Bo?" another youth taunted him. Bobo had to fire or fall back. He entered the store, alone, stopped at the candy case. Carolyn was behind the counter; Bobo in front. He asked for two cents' worth of bubble gum.

She handed it to him. He squeezed her hand and said: "How about a date, Baby?" She jerked away and started for Juanita Milam. At the break between counters, Bobo jumped in front of her, perhaps caught her at the waist, and said: "You needn't be afraid o' me, Baby. I been with white girls before." At this point, a cousin ran in, grabbed Bobo and began pulling him out of the store. Carolyn now ran, not for Juanita, but out the front, and got the pistol from the Milam car. Outside, with Bobo being ushered off by his cousins, and with Carolyn getting the gun, Bobo executed the "wolf whistle" which gave the case its name: **THE WOLF-WHISTLE MURDER: A NEGRO "CHILD" OR "BOY" WHISTLED AT HER AND THEY KILLED HIM.**

That was the sum of the facts on which most newspaper readers based an opinion. The Negroes drove away; and Carolyn, shaken, told Juanita. The two women determined to keep the incident from their "men-folks." They didn't tell J. W. Milam when he came to escort them home. By Thursday afternoon, Carolyn Bryant could see the story was getting around. She spent Thursday night at the Milam's, where at 4 a.m. (Friday) Roy got back from Texas. Since he had slept little for five nights, he went to bed at the Milams' while Carolyn returned to the store.

During Friday afternoon, Roy reached the store, and shortly thereafter a Negro told him what "the talk" was, and told him that the "Chicago boy" was "visitin' Preacher." Carolyn then told Roy what had happened. Once Roy Bryant knew, in his environment, in the opinion of most white people around him, for him to have done nothing would have marked him for a coward and a fool.

On Friday night, he couldn't do anything. He and Carolyn

were alone, and he had no car. Saturday was collection day, their busy day in the store. About 10:30 Saturday night, J. W. Milam drove by. Roy took him aside.

"I want you to come over early in the morning," he said. "I need a little transportation."

J.W. protested: "Sunday's the only morning I can sleep. Can't we make it around noon?"

Roy then told him.

"I'll be there," he said. "Early."

J. W. drove to another brother's store at Minter City, where he was working. He closed that store about 12:30 a.m., drove home to Glendora. Juanita was away, visiting her folks at Greenville. J. W. had been thinking. He decided not to go to bed. He pumped the pickup -- a half-ton '55 Chevrolet --full of gas and headed for Money.

J. W. "Big Milam" is 36; six feet two, 235 pounds; an extrovert. Short boots accentuate his height; khaki trousers; red sports shirt; sun helmet. Dark-visaged; his lower lip curls when he chuckles; and though bald, his remaining hair is jet-black. He is slavery's plantation overseer. Today, he rents Negro-driven mechanical cotton pickers to plantation owners. Those who know him say that he can handle Negroes better than anybody in the country.

Big Milam soldiered in the Patton manner. With a ninth-grade education, he was commissioned in battle by the 75th Division. He was an expert platoon leader, expert street fighter, expert in night patrol, expert with the "grease gun," with every device for close-range killing. A German bullet tore clear through his chest; his body bears "multiple shrapnel wounds." Of his medals, he cherishes one: combat infantryman's badge.

Big Milam, like many soldiers, brought home his favorite gun: the .45 Colt automatic pistol. "Best weapon the Army's got," he says. "Either for shootin' or sluggin'."

Two hours after Big Milam got the word -- the instant minute he could close the store -- he was looking for the Chicago Negro. Big Milam reached Money a few minutes shy of 2 a.m., Sunday, August 28. The Bryants were asleep; the store was dark but for the all-night light. He rapped at the back door, and when Roy came, he said: "Let's go. Let's make that trip now."

Roy dressed, brought a gun: this one was a .45 Colt. Both men were -- and remained -- cold sober. Big Milam had drunk a beer at Minter City around 9; Roy had had nothing. There was no moon as they drove to Preacher's house: 2.8 miles east of Money. Preacher's house stands 50 feet right of the gravel road, with cedar and persimmon trees in the yard. Big Milam drove the pickup in under the trees. He was bareheaded, carrying a five-cell flashlight in his left hand, the .45 in the right. Roy Bryant pounded on the door.

Preacher: "Who's that?"

Bryant: "Mr. Bryant, from Money, Preacher."

Preacher: "All right, sir. Just a minute."

Preacher came out of the screened-in porch.

Bryant: "Preacher, you got a boy from Chicago here?"

Preacher: "Yes sir."

Bryant: "I want to talk to him."

Preacher: "Yes sir. I'll get him."

Preacher led them to a back bedroom where four youths were sleeping in two beds. In one was Bobo

Till and Simeon Wright, Preacher's youngest son. Bryant had told Preacher to turn on the lights; Preacher had said they were out of order. So only the flashlight was used. The visit was not a complete surprise. Preacher testified that he had heard of the "trouble," that he "sho' had" talked to his nephew about it. Bobo himself had been afraid; he had wanted to go home the day after the incident. The Negro girl in the party urged that he leave.

"They'll kill him," she had warned. But Preacher's wife, Elizabeth Wright, had decided that the danger was being magnified; she had urged Bobo to "finish yo' visit."

"I thought they might say something to him, but I didn't think they'd kill a boy," Preacher said.

Milam: Big Milam shined the light in Bobo's face, said: "You the nigger who did the talking?"

Bobo: "Yeah," Bobo replied.

Milam: "Don't say, 'Yeah' to me: I'll blow your head off. Get your clothes on.'" Bobo had been sleeping in his shorts. He pulled on a shirt and trousers, then reached for his socks." Just the shoes," Milam hurried him

Bobo: "I don't wear shoes without socks," Bobo said; and he kept the gun-bearers waiting while he put on his socks, then a pair of canvas shoes with thick crepe soles. Preacher and his wife tried two arguments in the boy's behalf.

Preacher: "He ain't got good sense," Preacher begged. "He didn't know what he was doing. Don't take him."

"I'll pay you gentlemen for the damages," Elizabeth Wright said.

"You niggers go back to sleep," Milam replied.

They marched him into the yard, told him to get in the back of the pickup and lie down. He obeyed. They drove toward Money. Elizabeth Wright rushed to the home of a white neighbor, who got up, looked around, but decided he could do nothing. Then, she and Preacher drove to the home of her brother, Crosby Smith, at Sumner; and Crosby Smith, on Sunday morning, went to the sheriff's office at Greenwood. The other young Negroes stayed at Preacher's house until daylight, when Wheeler Parker telephoned his mother in Chicago, who in turn notified Bobo's mother, Mamie Bradley, 33, 6427 S. St. Lawrence.

Had there been any doubt as to the identity of the "Chicago boy who done the talking," Milam and Bryant would have stopped at the store for Carolyn to identify him. But there had been no denial. So they didn't stop at the store. At Money, they crossed the Tallahatchie River and drove west. Their intention was to "just whip him... and scare some sense into him." And for this chore, Big Milam knew "the scariest place in the Delta." He had come upon it last year hunting wild geese. Over close to Rosedale, the Big River bends around under a bluff. "Brother, she's a 100-foot sheer drop, and she's a 100 feet deep after you hit." Big Milam's idea was to stand him up there on that bluff, "whip" him with the .45, and then shine the light on down there toward that water and make him think you're gonna knock him in.

"Brother, if that won't scare the Chicago -------, hell won't."

Searching for this bluff, they drove close to 75 miles. Through Shellmound, Schlater, Doddsville, Ruleville, Cleveland, to the intersection south of Rosedale. There they turned south on Mississippi No. 1, toward the entrance to Beulah Lake. They tried several dirt and gravel roads, drove along the levee. Finally, they gave up: in the darkness, Big Milam couldn't find his bluff. They drove back to Milam's house at Glendora, and by now it was 5 a.m. They had been driving nearly three hours, with Milam and Bryant in the cab and Bobo lying in the back.

At some point when the truck slowed down, why hadn't Bobo jumped and run? He wasn't tied; nobody was holding him. A partial answer is that those Chevrolet pickups have a wraparound rear window the size of a windshield. Bryant could watch him. But the real answer is the remarkable part of the story. Bobo wasn't afraid of them! He was tough as they were. He didn't think they had the guts to kill him.

Milam: "We were never able to scare him. They had just filled him so full of that poison that he was hopeless."

Back of Milam's home is a tool house, with two rooms each about 12 feet square. They took him in there and began "whipping" him, first Milam, then Bryant smashing him across the head with those .45's. Pistol-whipping: a court-martial offense in the Army... but MP's have been known to do it.... And Milam got information out of German prisoners this way. But under these blows Bobo never hollered -- and he kept making the perfect speeches to insure martyrdom.

Bobo: "You bastards, I'm not afraid of you. I'm as good as you are. I've 'had' white women. My grandmother was a white woman."

Milam: "Well, what else could we do? He was hopeless. I'm no bully; I never hurt a nigger in my life. I like niggers -- in their place -- I know how to work 'em. But I just decided it was time a few people got put on notice. As long as I live and can do anything about it, niggers are gonna stay in their place.

Niggers ain't gonna vote where I live. If they did, they'd control the government. They ain't gonna go to school with my kids. And when a nigger gets close to mentioning sex with a white woman, he's tired o' livin'. I'm likely to kill him. Me and my folks fought for this country, and we've got some rights. I stood there in that shed and listened to that nigger throw that poison at me, and I just made up my mind. 'Chicago boy,' I said, 'I'm tired of 'em sending your kind down here to stir up trouble. Goddam you, I'm going to make an example of you -- just so everybody can know how me and my folks stand.'"

So big Milam decided to act. He needed a weight. He tried to think of where he could get an anvil. Then he remembered a gin which had installed new equipment. He had seen two men lifting a discarded fan, a metal fan three feet high and circular, used in ginning cotton. Bobo wasn't bleeding much. Pistol-whipping bruises more than it cuts. They ordered him back in the truck and headed west again. They passed through Doddsville, went to the Progressive Ginning Company. This gin is 3.4 miles east of Boyle: Boyle is two miles south of Cleveland. The road to this gin turns left off U.S. 61, after you cross the bayou bridge south of Boyle.

Milam: "When we got to that gin, it was daylight, and I was worried for the first time. Somebody might see us and accuse us of stealing the fan."

Bryant and Big Milam stood aside while Bobo loaded the fan. Weight: 74 pounds. The youth still thought they were bluffing. They drove back to Glendora, then north toward Swan Lake and crossed the "new bridge" over the Tallahatchie. At the east end of this bridge, they turned right, along a dirt road which parallels the river. After about two miles, they crossed the property of L.W. Boyce, passing near his house. About 1.5 miles southeast of the Boyce home is a lonely spot where Big Milam has hunted squirrels. The river bank is steep. The truck stopped 30 yards from the water. Big Milam ordered Bobo to pick up the fan. He staggered under its weight... carried it to the river bank. They stood silently... just hating one another.

Milam: "Take off your clothes."

Slowly, Bobo pulled off his shoes, his socks. He stood up, unbuttoned his shirt, dropped his pants, his sh**orts.** He stood there naked. It was Sunday morning, a little before 7.

Milam: "You still as good as I am?"

Bobo: "Yeah."

Milam: "You still 'had' white women?"

Bobo: "Yeah."

That big .45 jumped in Big Milam's hand. The youth turned to catch that big expanding bullet at his right ear. He dropped. They barb-wired the gin fan to his neck, rolled him into 20 feet of water. For three hours that morning, there was a fire in Big Milam's back yard: Bobo's crepe-soled shoes were hard to burn. Seventy-two hours later -- eight miles downstream -- boys were fishing. They saw feet sticking out of the water. It was Bobo.

The majority—by no means all, but the majority—of the white people in Mississippi 1) either approve Big Milam's actions or else 2) they don't disapprove enough to risk giving their "enemies" the satisfaction of a conviction.

END

Mother of Emmett Till at the funeral of her son who was brutally murdered.

Uncle of Emmett Till, Moses Wright's house, East Money, Mississippi. Till was kidnapped from this home by several white men and murdered in 1955

Moses Wright holding his nephews Emmett Till's trousers.

CHRISTIAN SCIENCE MONITOR
May 12, 1959, pg. 13

OFFICIAL DROPPED BY NAACP CHIEFS FOR VIOLENCE BID.

[By the Associated Press, New York]
A suspended official of the National Association for the Advancement of Colored People told reporters on May 11, that southern Negroes should carry arms. Robert F. Williams, a former combat marine, was suspended by NAACP executive secretary Roy Wilkins on May 6 for urging southern Negroes to "fight violence with violence." Mr. Williams had been president of the Union County, N.C. branch of the NAACP.

The NAACP's board of directors, with 18 of its 48 members present, on May 11 voted in support of Mr. Wilkins, maintaining the association has always opposed violence. At a news conference, Mr. Williams stuck to his stand. "Negroes, as a matter of forethought, must be ready to carry arms to combat violence," he said. "When you have strength of force to bargain with, it becomes a matter of mutual security for both whites and Negroes." He said he would demand that the NAACP adopt a policy calling for its members to "defend themselves with arms if necessary."

Mr. Williams said he was not advocating that Negroes lynch a white man each time a Negro is lynched. Mr. Williams said southern Negroes must go to federal courts to obtain justice in racial matters. He said he did not expect they would receive any justice in racial matters from state or local courts in the South.

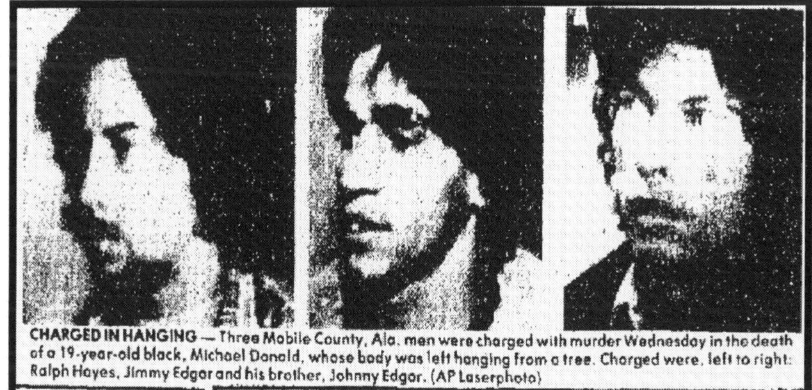

CHARGED IN HANGING — Three Mobile County, Ala. men were charged with murder Wednesday in the death of a 19-year-old black, Michael Donald, whose body was left hanging from a tree. Charged were, left to right: Ralph Hayes, Jimmy Edgar and his brother, Johnny Edgar. (AP Laserphoto)

Alton Telegraph (Illinois) - March 26, 1981, "CHARGED IN HANGING — Three Mobile County, Ala. men were charged with murder Wednesday in the death of a 19-year-o d black Michael Donald, whose body was left hanging from a tree. Charged were, left to right: Ralph Hayes, Jimmy Edgar and his brother, Johnny Edgar. (AP laser photo)"

CHRONICLE TELEGRAM (ELYRIA, OHIO)
March 26, 1981

ARREST OF 3 WHITES EASES RACIAL TENSIONS IN MOBILE.

MOBILE, Ala. (UPI.) —The arrest of three white men on murder charges appears to have ceased rising tensions in the black community since the body of a 19-year-old black man was found hanging from a tree limb.

The three suspects, two of them ex-convicts, were arrested Wednesday and held without bond in the death of Michael Donald. Police refused to discuss the motive, saying it would jeopardize their case. Earl Shinhoster, southeast regional director of the NAACP in Atlanta, called on Attorney General William French Smith to "initiate a federal civil rights investigation into the lynching."

TECHNICALLY, Donald, a masonry student, was not lynched. An autopsy revealed he was dead—beaten and strangled—before he was strung up in an elm tree in a racially mixed neighborhood. His body was found Saturday.

C. Edwin Enright, special agent in charge of the FBI's Mobile office, said federal agents would continue providing technical assistance to local police but said no decision has been made on a federal investigation.

"We have been following this investigation since it started and the results of our monitoring have been channeled to the Department of Justice," said Enright. "They will make the decision on whether to involve the federal government. I have no idea when that decision will be made."

CHARGED WERE: Ralph Hayes 23, a pulpwood worker, Jimmy Edgar, 22, and his brother Johnny Edgar, 26. Hayes lived across the street from where Donald was found and policed said both he and the younger Edgar had prison records. All three were to be arraigned April 2.

CHRONICLE TELEGRAM (ELYRIA, OHIO)
March 28, 1981

FUNERAL OF LYNCHED TEEN GUARDED.

MOBILE, Ala., (UPI)—Police put extra patrols in the streets today to guard against possible violence during the funeral of a black teen-ager who was beaten, strangled, and then hanged from an elm tree.

"We'll put a few more people out just to be ready if anything happens," Mobile Mayor Robert Doyle said. State Sen. Michael Figures, a local civil rights leader, said the funeral home handling the body of Michael Donald, 19, had received some threatening telephone calls and "we expect security to be there" at the funeral. Three white men described by police as "street toughs" have been charged with Donald's death.

Michael Donald killed by United Klans of America (KKK),

Mobile, Alabama, March 20, 1981.

KKK postcard cartoon depicting a black man being hung. Postcard was used as evidence in the civil trial resulting from Michael Donald's murder.

PACIFIC STARS & STRIPES VIEWPOINT (TOKYO, JAPAN) [U.S. Military Newspaper]
February 27, 1987

LYNCH MOB MENTALITY IS STILL WITH US.

BOCA RATON, Fla.—It was a gruesome crime, as most lynchings are. Some members of the United Klans of America simply seized 19-year-old Michael Donald at random, as he walked along a street in Mobile, Alabama. The Klansmen beat Donald with a tree limb, strangled him, slit his throat, and then left him hanging from a tree in a racially integrated neighborhood. What was this 1981 lynching all about? James "Tiger" Knowles, a 24-year-old Klansman who has been sentenced to life in prison for his role in the murder, has testified that the goal was to intimidate blacks, warning them not to serve on juries, and to let everyone know how strong the Klan was in Alabama.

That heinous crime did create fear among blacks—deep worries that they were moving into another cycle in which lynchings became a sort of spectator sport, like dogfights. But, blacks soon saw evidence that the South and the nation had changed profoundly, even from the post-World War II period when the Klan and lynchings became resurgent. In the 1940s, lynchers were rarely indicted, and if charged, generally acquitted. This time there were indictments, and not only was Knowles sentenced to life, but another Klansman, 32-year-old Henry Francis Hays, was convicted and sentenced to death. Then, just this month, a federal jury in Mobile assessed $7 million in damages against the United Klans of America and six past and present Klansmen.

A lawyer for the Donald family called it a "landmark ruling that would make sure Donald's death was the last Klan lynching." I wonder. Some Klansmen say the convictions and the $7 million judgment will only provoke thousands more whites to flock to the Klan. One thing we know: The lynch mob mentality has never vanished in America.

The recent racial tragedy in Howard Beach, N.Y., was a lynching, pure and simple. A mob of white teen-agers beat blacks with bats and tree limbs and then, unable to string anyone up in a tree, chased one black man onto a roadway where he was run over by a car. The teen-age mob was teaching blacks not to come into their neighborhood, even to eat pizza. Again, the difference between now and a quarter century ago is that there are indictments. A jury will decide who is guilty of murder, lesser crimes, or nothing in this killing. Still, in New York, as in Alabama, some people are throwing around ugly warnings that the "harsh" indictments will only create more racial hostility.

These threats are worrisome to anyone who notes another element of change since the 1940s. Time was when black people got lynched only if accused of raping (or at least whistling at) a white woman. Now blacks are being lynched for daring to vote, serve on a jury, move freely about a city, or otherwise exercise basic rights of citizenship. Is this really progress? Does this really give us reason to believe that Klansmen in Alabama or teen-agers in New York have perpetuated their last lynching?

I wish I could believe that lynch law is finally consigned to America's past. But I don't. Americans who refuse to be governed by mobs, in or out of hoods and bed sheets, are going to have to be more vigilant, and uncompromising than ever before if we are to escape the national shame engendered by mob murders.

THE END

(AP) Photo of James Byrd Jr.

(AP) Photo The bumper of the 1982 pickup truck used to drag James Byrd Jr. to his death is shown in Jasper, Texas.

(AP) Photo ***Spray paint marks the spot where officials found the head of James Byrd, a 49-year-old black man, along Huff Creek Road near Jasper, Texas. Byrd was tied to a truck and dragged to his death along the rural East Texas road in the early morning hours of June 7, 1998.***

GOV. ROLPH

15487965R00119

Printed in Great Britain
by Amazon